Growing Up
Southern

Growing Up

Southern

SOUTHERN EXPOSURE LOOKS AT CHILDHOOD, THEN AND NOW

EDITED BY
Chris Mayfield

PANTHEON BOOKS
New York

Grateful acknowledgment is made to the following for permission to reprint
previously published material:

The Continuum Publishing Corporation: Excerpt from *Brother to a Dragonfly* by
Will D. Campbell. Published by The Seabury Press, Inc.
New Republic Books: Excerpt from *What My Heart Wants to Tell* by Verna Mae
Slone. Copyright © 1979 by Verna Mae Slone. Published by New Republic
Books, Washington, D.C.

Library of Congress Cataloging in Publication Data

Main entry under title:

Growing up southern.

    1.   Southern States—Social life and customs—
1865–   —Addresses, essays, lectures. 2.   Children—
I. Mayfield, Chris. II. Southern exposure.
F215.G86   975   80–8658
ISBN 0–394–50913–7
ISBN 0–394–74809–3 (pbk.)

Designed by Clint Anglin

Manufactured in the United States of America

First Edition

Contents

v

Introduction

CHRIS MAYFIELD

"GROWING UP SOUTHERN"
. . . The words evoke a tide of images, both bitter and sweet: overalls and organdy, hot green fields, cool brown creeks, Grandma's front porch, lengthy and complicated family connections, Mama's fried chicken and biscuits and Granddaddy's cane syrup, "colored" water fountains and "white" ones, church, chores, Dixie, and hot dark dangerous summer nights.

Today's Southern children get their biscuits as often from Hardee's as from Mama. On Saturday afternoons they're as likely to cool off in the local shopping mall as in a shady spring-fed swimming hole. But Grandma and Grandpa and Uncle Joe and Cudn Elaine loom large in the lives of today's Southern kids, just as they did in those of earlier generations. The hard work many children still do isn't likely to be acknowledged by their elders; "colored" and "white" labels are less blatant, but they still constrict the futures of this generation's Southern children. *Growing Up Southern* explores the continuities and the chasms between the lives of Southern children today and in the past.

As is our tradition at *Southern Exposure,* we've chosen whenever possible to let our subjects speak for themselves. The rising interest in oral history has served us well here. Mrs. Mamie Garvin Fields—at 92, our oldest living narrator—tells of a proud tradition of self-education and

ix

resistance to the Jim Crow laws in a Charleston family
around the turn of the century. In "Mill Village Memories,"
we hear of the security and the homemade backyard fun
which small children enjoyed in a pre-World War I mill
town; we see also how these same youngsters knocked
their heads against the ceiling of constricted opportunity as
they entered the twelve-hour-a-day world of mill work,
when they were as young as six or eight years old. "We all
worked, and we got what we could," says Sara Brooks, the
daughter of an Alabama freeholder, speaking of her
childhood on the farm during the 1920s. "Everything that
we ate, we mostly raised it ourselves." Again and again,
our older narrators talk about their hard work, the close
family ties, the importance of church and community, the
treasured simple pleasures, the limitations and the
self-sufficiency which they remember as part of Southern
childhood the way it used to be.

We had to work harder to find ways to let today's
Southern youngsters speak for themselves. Few kids write
lengthy memoirs; few have oral historians standing at their
elbows with tape recorders and eager questions. In "Our
Town," however, elementary school children talk to their
interviewer/friend/teacher Nathalie Andrews about the
places and people of their close-knit urban-Appalachian
neighborhood in Louisville, Kentucky. Alma Blount
photographed and interviewed a gang of teenagers at their
late-night hangout in back of a large shopping mall,
revealing a stereotypical alienation, but also a strong and
collective culture.

Traditionally, Southerners have—for good reasons and
bad—resisted government control over their lives, and
especially over their children's lives. Public schools took
hold in many parts of the South later than in other regions
of the country; desegregation of public schools has been
the bitterest battle in the South since the Civil War.
Ironically, and mainly because of their poverty, more
children in the South than anywhere else are controlled by
the gigantic and inefficient foster-care system which Lanier
Rand Holt and Jennifer Miller describe in "Ending
Foster-Care Drift." Besides the horror stories of millions of
children lost in foster-care "drift," the article shows the

system's inherent biases against poor families and how these biases reappear in new forms among the middle-class reformers now seeking to ensure a permanent home for each child in state custody.

Day care is another way in which Southern families are surrendering their children to the care of others, and the options here are depressingly bleak. Although most working parents in the region still make informal arrangements for child care with their relatives or friends, the world of day-care centers is growing rapidly. In several articles, we examine from the inside what it's like to grow up and to work in day care; we look at the good and bad ways in which day care, as it currently exists, differs from growing up at home. Finally, we offer some suggestions for how day care *could* work, if we—as communities, as a region, and as a nation—gave it the attention that it so urgently deserves.

It's easy to romanticize the beauties of the past and denigrate the realities of the present. The many photographs we present of today's Southern children— poignant, funny, sad, joyous, and above all beautiful—are evidence enough that we don't believe the latest generation of Southerners has gone to the dogs. In addition, we've gathered a variety of the children's own writings, drawings, and photographs, through which they speak eloquently—if sometimes cryptically, or through a wry corner of the mouth—of their lives and of the multiplicity of experience which still marks growing up Southern. Though kids may watch hours of TV and hang out in plastic food franchises, for many of them deep roots in family, community, and landscape remain central and shaping forces. The children in Beaufort County, South Carolina, reveal imaginations as gothic as that of any Southern novelists as they describe the "ghost trees and swishing winds" of their low country. Robert Cooper's young photography students in West Virginia share with us their beautiful, impoverished mountain community: one self-portrait shows an eleven-year-old girl with a round face and long thick pigtails posed before her family's TV, sheltering a brood of young children with her arms. In another, someone's grandfather stands as thin and erect as the skinny apple tree he's pruning. We see animals, work boots, clotheslines, pictures of Jesus, and in all the photos we appreciate what teacher Robert Cooper describes as the "moods of quiet contemplation and youthful exuberance" in which the children used their cameras.

Racism and race consciousness are two themes which run throughout this volume, as they do throughout Southern life. Nowhere do the changes, and the grounds for hope, come through more clearly than in the short stories by eight-year-old Dorothy Williams and twelve-year-old Honoree Jeffers. Separated in time by forty-two years and an era's changes in circumstance, these two little girls share an unusual narrative gift and a hilarious delight in exaggeration and melodrama. Dorothy Williams wrote during the Depression years in south Georgia, and her story describes a "white little girl's" nightmare of being "snatched into a strange house by a strange woman" and made to wash endless piles of other people's dirty dishes— a task reserved for little black girls. Finally, the heroine is rescued by a "blessed man," who tells her tormentor that "she shouldn't have white little girls for maids."

Dorothy Williams had little opportunity to think otherwise than in these racist terms. But four decades later, Honoree Jeffers gleefully rewrites history, freed from those constraints. Her historical fiction—a slavery-times soap opera from a 1980s black perspective—emphasizes the gullibility of the white owners and the cleverness and bravery of the slaves: "White people never saw through the armor of blacks. . . . Martha hated and scorned blacks who *really* meant all that nonsense about bowing and scraping."

We hope you'll laugh, snicker, cuss, think, worry, recoil, exclaim, and remember as you turn the pages of *Growing Up Southern*. And we hope you'll look with new respect and higher expectations at the Southerners growing up today.

A Note on the Poetry

THE POETRY THAT MARKS the interludes between the sections of this book was all written by Southern youngsters in recent years. The poems come from three sources: a remedial reading classroom for sixth and seventh graders taught by Marjorie Mayfield in Wadley, Georgia; the Imagine creative writing program in Durham, North Carolina; and the Poetry in the Schools program in Beaufort County, South Carolina, directed by Dr. Thomas McClanahan.

These young writers generally stand outside the elite groups of academic achievers in their schools. Most are poor and/or black; they come more often from remedial programs than from groups for gifted children. Yet the beauty and power of their language defy every stereotype of cultural deprivation propagated in academic circles. The poems are proof that poverty and bad schools do not in themselves doom children to dullness and incoherence. Many teachers have found the opposite situation, that the educational process in this country too often blunts rather than sharpens children's individuality and their powers of perception and artistic expression. Often, the poorer a child's academic performance, the more likely he or she is to scrawl out a fabulous poem. But few teachers have the time, the freedom, or the patience to preside over the slow mining of these diamonds in the rough.

"Visiting artists are amazed," says Tom McClanahan, speaking of his poetry program in South Carolina's isolated, poverty-stricken coastal low country, "at the children's receptivity to strange new ideas. They agree that the quality of the children's creative work is nothing less than astounding. The children draw richly on the imagery of the surrounding low-country environment of swamps, pine trees, Spanish moss, snakes, fish and, of course, the ocean."

This is not to argue in favor of poverty and ineffective education as a means of producing fine artists. The tragedy is that our schools so seldom recognize or build on the unique strengths which many Southern children bring unnoticed into the classroom: the strong family and community ties, the magic of the natural landscape, the self-sufficiency born of need, the legacy of humor and tradition, and regional patterns of speech. None of these gifts can be measured by competency tests or SATs. They are precious and perhaps fragile resources, vulnerable to erosion by the tides of mass-media culture and consumerism. Schools could act as bulwarks to shore up and defend resources; children could be helped to view the images of the "normal" foisted upon them by television and other standardizing forces with skepticism and humor rather than with feelings of self-pity and inadequacy. The children whose poems we present here are inspiring examples of how this process can work.

Growing Up Southern

Interlude

Dale
CLASS POEM, GRADE 5, DALE ELEMENTARY

Quiet, a dead town
All you see is gnats and skeeters
Folks hoe the field
Ghost trees like a swishing wind
White church like a spook house
full of bats and vampires,
skeletons playing piano
All getting up on their graves
Worms coming out of the eye
Bones from dinosaurs, years ago
Ponds with grass and water moccasins
that hang like slime on a pine tree;
That reminds me of a Witch
while bluebirds fly and buzzards eat
the eyes of dead dogs. . . .

The Sea
RICKY MCARTHUR, GRADE 6,
BATTERY CREEK ELEMENTARY

The sea roared and the fire raged out of control
The city blazed and the earth cracked.
The sea sank.
It was something like a draining tank.
Now, it's all over and the world is gone
* and very contented.*

The Beautiful Castle

ANGIE PERRY, AGE 11

*Once upon a time there was an old man named Mr.
Winter. He stayed by himself, and a grandson
stayed with him every night. His wife died in his
bed. Mr. Winter was so scared he dreamed about
his wife every night. She had a stroke.*

*So Mr. Winter cooked every night. The little
boy, he went around selling cookies for the old
man to have some money to buy some food.
His mama used to sell them.*

*When all the food was gone, they went to
the store and sold some bottles for five cents. They
hung a magic bottle from the ceiling and it turned
into a magic castle. They would always have food
and money in the castle.*

*When the boy got to be about thirty-nine years old, he
found a wife to marry. His grandfather and his wife
and him lived in the castle. It was made out of
glass. They was so rich. They had all the money in
the world.*

ONE

They Were Educated Without Blows

M. LEPAGE DU PRATZ, *HISTORY OF LOUISIANA,* 1774

WHEN ANY OF THE women of the natives is delivered, she goes immediately to the water and washes herself and the infant; she then comes home and lies down, after having disposed her infant in the cradle, which is about two feet and a half long, nine inches broad and half a foot deep, being formed of straight pieces of cane bent up at one end, to serve for a foot or stay.

When the boys are about twelve years of age, they are given a bow and arrows proportioned to their strength, and in order to exercise them they tie some hay, about twice as large as the fist, to the end of a pole about ten feet high. He who brings down the hay receives the prize from an old man who is always present: the best shooter is called the young warrior; the next best is called the apprentice warrior; and so on of the others, who are prompted to excel more by sentiments of honor than by blows.

If any of their young people happen to fight, which I never saw nor heard during the whole time I resided in their neighborhood, they threaten to put them in a hut at a great distance from their nation, as persons unworthy to live among others; and this is repeated to them so often, that if they happen to have had a battle, they take care never to have another. I have already observed that I studied them a considerable number

of years, and I never could learn that there were ever any
disputes or boxing matches among either their boys or
men.

As the children grow up, the fathers and mothers take
care each to accustom those of their own sex to the labors
and exercises suited to them, and they have no great
trouble to keep them employed; but it must be confessed
that the girls and the women work more than the men and
the boys. These last go to a hunting and fishing, cut the
wood, the smallest bits of which are carried home by the
women; they clear the fields for corn, and hoe it; and on
days when they cannot go abroad they amuse themselves
with making, after their fashion, pick-axes, oars, paddles
and other instruments, which once made last a long while.
The women on the other hand have their children to bring
up, have to pound the maize for the subsistence of the
family, have to keep up the fire and to make a great many
utensils, which require a good deal of work and last but a
short time, such as their earthen ware, their matts, their
clothes and a thousand other things of that kind.

The boys and girls, from the time they are three years of
age, are called out every morning by an old man, to go to
the river; and here is some more employment for the
mothers who accompany them thither to teach them to
swim. Those who can swim tolerable well make a great
noise in winter by beating the water in order to frighten
away the crocodiles, and keep themselves warm.

The reader will have observed that most of the labor and
fatigue falls to the share of the women; but I can declare
that I never heard them complain of their fatigues, unless of
the trouble their children gave them, which complaint
arose as much from maternal affection as from any
attention that the children required. The girls from their
infancy have it instilled into them that if they are sluttish or
unhandy they will have none but a dull awkward fellow for
their husband; I observed in all the nations I visited, that
this threatening was never lost upon the young girls.

I would not have it thought, however, that the young
men are altogether idle. Their occupations indeed are not
of such a long continuance; but they are much more

laborious. As the men have occasion for more strength, reason requires that they should not exhaust themselves in their youth; but at the same time they are not exempted from those exercises that fit them for war and hunting. The children are educated without blows; and the body is left at full liberty to grow, and to form and strengthen itself with their years.

They have still, I allow, a great deal more spare time than the women; but this is not all thrown away. As these people have not the assistance of writing, they are obliged to have recourse to tradition, in order to preserve the remembrance of any remarkable transactions; and this tradition cannot be learned but by frequent repetitions; consequently many of the youths are often employed in hearing the old men narrate the history of their ancestors, which is thus transmitted from generation to generation. In order to preserve their traditions pure and uncorrupt, they are careful not to deliver them indifferently to all their young people, but teach them only to those young men of whom they have the best opinion.

TWO

You May Plow Here

SARA BROOKS AND THORDIS SIMONSEN

BORN IN WEST-CENTRAL Alabama in 1911, Sara Brooks was raised on a farm her father owned. Freeholding was not common among blacks of Will Brooks's generation, but Will Brooks was an uncommon man. As a boy he worked for wages, and a few years later he rented some land which he farmed in return for a share of the harvest. But Mr. Brooks was committed to land ownership. One year he made a good crop, saved one bale of cotton until prices rose, and applied the profits to the purchase of the farm where Sara grew up.

Will Brooks married for the first time in 1907, when he was about twenty-three. Three children were born, but the middle one died, leaving Davey and Sara. Mr. Brooks remarried six years after he was widowed, and more children came into the family. He managed to support everyone by "taking in" more land. He plowed, put down fertilizer, and planted his crops —all with the help of his family.

When Sara Brooks's brother and her two older cousins, whom her father raised, had all married and left home, Sara "knew all the big work was gonna be on me," so she married and left. But then she farmed with her husband. When their marriage ended, she did factory work and housework in Mobile, where her sister lived. Finally, she joined her brother in Cleveland, where she works and lives today.

WHEN WE COME HOME FROM SCHOOL, WE'D PULL OFF
our gingham dresses what we'd wear to school each day,
and we would put on our old work dresses that we used to
work in the summer and go into the tater bank and get us
some raw sweet potatoes. Oh, I used to love to eat raw
potatoes! Crunch, crunch, crunch. Sweet potatoes! We
grew red and white sweet potatoes, and Irish potatoes, and
cabbage and collards and turnip greens—we grew all that
in the garden. Momma had a fenced-in garden right by the
well where she'd have her strawberries; she grew garlic
and onions, and what else she had in there? Butter beans,
they are always raised in the garden around the palings
'cause they grew on the palings. And mustard greens, beets,
radishes, and string beans and English peas. Oh, and we had
tomatoes in the garden. They'd be laying down everywhere

—just pretty red ripe tomatoes. And we had peach trees and purple plums in the garden. We had Alberta peach trees in the garden, and the seeds fall under the tree and they would come up and my mother would set out little ones. They'll grow.

And we had fields away from the house that was bigger than that, where we raised peanuts and corn and millet, ribbon cane and some cotton. All these was raised away from the house. You could look for just I don't know how far, and it'd be so pretty with the cotton be so level all the way across, and then it goes to the cornfields, and then the cornfield is high all the way across. It was beautiful; it really was. And we had a lot. Everything that we ate mostly, we raised it ourselves, except our sugar and our flour. We had some farm!

We raised our own chickens and our own hogs— sometime be twelve, fifteen of them hogs running around. And we had cows; we had a lotta cows, which we milked every day. Then we had turkeys we'd kill at Christmas time. And guineas we had; guineas always was around the house. The guineas be "pot-rack, pot-rack, pot-rack." That's what the guineas say. And the old turkey be "gobble, gobble," and the roosters be "coo *coo* coo *coo.*" We always had plenty to eat, and it was busy, you know. Something's always going on on the farm.

The first house that we lived in was a *two-roomed* house. And it had one chimney, and that one chimney made two fireplaces, one in each room. No one lived there then but my father, my brother, and my grandmother and me. My father and Davey slept in one room, and my grandmother and me slept in the other room; I slept in the same bed with my grandmother.

I don't even remember when my mother died because I was only nine months old. My grandmother raised me from nine months old until I was six, and I didn't know that she wasn't my *mother* until my father's fixing to marry. I was around five or six years old.

My father only by that time had three children, but one of them had died; there was me—I'm the baby—and the oldest one, because the middle one had died with meningitis. And then I was raised by my father and my stepmother, which was a *very,* very sweet lady. This good stepmother raised me and my brother, then she had nine children of her own, but we all seem as whole sisters and brothers because they loved us and they gave us all that they were able to give us.

We all worked hard, and we got what we could. And my father took care of all the family. He'd taken care of his grandmother until she died; then he taken care of his mother until she passed. Then he took his sister's children and raised them right along with me; it was two of them, Rhoda and Molly. Then he taken care of his crippled brother, which was named Jim, until he passed. My father did all this.

My father would start breaking up the land in March. He would be plowing by himself—he'd plow from sunup to sundown—and the only company that he really had was listening to the birds. Whatever it sound like the bird say, he would put it into words. He was plowing one day at a low place and a bird was singing when he was plowing and he made a song from what the bird sung:

You may plow here, just as much as you please. You may plow here, just as deep as your knees. But I will tell you, right before your face, You ain't goin' make nothin' here But burrs and weeds, But burrs and weeds.

He worked every day, and we had our little house. And from time to time, he had more built onto this two-roomed house. When he got married, he had an addition put on this house, which was the kitchen and a dining room. Then he bought a stove, an iron stove with a reservoir to it. And when the family began to expand and was getting bigger, my daddy kept adding more to this house till we had a kitchen, a dining room, and a company room—for the

company if the company came (we keeped that room closed every day until Sunday)—and three bedrooms and a porch. That's where we was raised up.

We lived in the country, and we wasn't living really close around anyone. So we'd love to get out; we'd get out and go to church in order to go someplace. Our church didn't have a meeting but once a month, so we'd stay at our church those Sundays. And if our church didn't have a meeting that Sunday, we'd leave our Sunday school and go to another church. We'd go to Trimble first Sunday; second Sunday we'd go to Horizon; third Sunday we'd go to Pleasantville; and the fourth Sunday we'd go to the Methodist church, see?

So we went. Some Sundays we walked. That was a *long* walk. We started early, and sometime somebody passing in a wagon would pick us up, and we'd go. And when my daddy went—he was dutiful about going to church—he would drive the wagon or we'd be riding in the surrey. And when we walked, we went barefeeted. And it seemed like nothing to walk, 'cause I used to like to cross the streams and stop and play in them; I did. And sometime we'd get to church and my feet be wet because I'd went in the water—you know how kids do. But we taken us in a bag a wet towel, and when we get near the church, we'd wipe all the dust off our feet and legs and put on our shoes and our stockings and go on to church. Going back, when we got to a certain distance, we'd pull 'em off and go on home. And we be sittin around weepin over the next day counta gotta go to school or go to work.

In the mornings, getting up, my father would call Rhoda first. "Rhoda, get up. Rhoda, get up! It's time to get up!" And Rhoda say, "Yes, sir, Uncle Will." And that's when Rhoda'd get the rest of us up, 'cause I'd hear it too because she and I and Molly slept together, so we all waked up by the same time. But I'd make like I was asleep. I wouldn't say *nothing*. I would be the last one to get up if it's possible. We stayed in bed long as we could, but we had to be up before six, because if we were going to field, we had to get up and cook.

We'd get up, and you make up your bed and go wash up and get ready to get in the kitchen. Whoever's gonna cook, cooked; and the other two would go to the cowpen and milk the cows. Then we would come from the cowpen, strain the milk, put the milk in the churn, wash out the strainer and things, and hang them up. Then we's ready for breakfast.

For breakfast we'd usually have butter and biscuits and syrup and milk. We didn't have meat, because in the summertime the meat would be about out—it wouldn't be no good to eat. We'd have breakfast; then we's all ready to go to field.

We'd be going to field sometime at good daybreak, so we'd work a lots before it gets too hot, you know what I mean? The sun would be so hot you could see little devils, you know, little things twinkling out in front of you when it be real hot. Little things—they just quiver. We called 'em "lazy jacks." It was the heat.

We'd take our hoe on our shoulder, and we'd have on our straw hats, and we'd be chopping corn or chopping cotton. That's what we'd be doing in the summer. Or we'd be hoeing peanuts—we had to keep the grass cleaned out. And, oh, the rows'ld be so long! To be in the field hoeing, it was awful to look from one end of the row to the other after the sun gets hot. In the morning time, or in the evening, when you know it's getting near time to go home, you never think nothing about it. But when it was hot in the day and the devils would be showing, the rows were *long.*

We never had no time off; we always worked up until twelve o'clock. And when we's working in the field, we never knew what time it would be. So we'd stand the hoe up, and if the shadow of that hoe gets short, you know it's getting along near twelve o'clock. When that hoe is standing on its shadow, you know it's noontime.

So we'd go under a tree and sit down. We had lotta trees around, 'cause whenever it rained, that's where we went—under the trees and stood. My mother'd bring dinner to the field, and we'd eat under the trees. She'd bring one big bucket of peas, and then in another one she'd have greens. Cabbage greens or collard greens—she's gonna boil a pot every day. And we'd have cornbread. Then sometimes she'd bring milk she'd maybe churned

before dinner. And we had meat, big old hunk of boiled meat. Some of the little ones would come, too, and help bring the dinner. To top it off, we'd always have some sweet; we'd have syrup bread or we'd have some kinda pie or another—big old apple pie, berry pie, or peach pie. It was real good. So we'd eat our dinner, and then, when we get through eating, we just rest awhile. And then we go right back to work.

My father come around pretty often when we's working in the field. He was always watching. And when we'd be done got tired—we kinda not working so hard, and we getting around too slow—he would tell us all, "Listen at that bird." The birds would be singing. "You know what that bird saying?" We'd say, "No." He'd say, "That bird saying, 'Laziness'll kill you,' so let's get going."

But we never was lazy, 'cause we used to really work.

Oh, fight sometime, fuss sometime, but worked on. Sometime we'd stay in the field until about five o'clock in the evening. Then we'd come home, and we didn't have too much to do in the summer when we come home but just to feed the hogs and milk the cows. So when we come in from work, we'd step on the back porch and wash up on our way in. Then we'd go eat. Then we washed the dishes and all and get through doing that. And if it was summertime, we'd take some chairs out on the porch at night and we'd sing. It was my two cousins and the smaller kids what was coming up under us and my brother. Oh boy! We used to have a good choir. Really! It really sound good. You could hear our voices going way out at night. And then we'd sing so, some peoples over farther from us would hear us, and they'd sing. You see, that's the only entertainment we *really* had. These times these kids are having now, they think is good. It's nothing, just nothing, really. And we hear the frogs; they'd be "whoop-whoop, whoop-whoop" down there in the woods. It was so quiet and everything.

When Saturday night come, that was the really big bath night. Before you go to bed, you take your Saturday night bath because you getting ready to go out for Sunday. Our bathtub was a tin tub, and we took our bath in the bedroom where we slept. We carried warm water from the stove and put it in the tub; the stove had a reservoir on it what we kept water hot on one side, but you wouldn't have a whole lot of it. Sometime in the summertime we set the big tub outside and we'd draw water from the well and we'd leave the water in the tub. Then when we come home in the evening, it was just nice enough to take a bath in it without heating it.

ON SUNDAYS, I WORE BABY DOLL SHOES. IT'S A STRAP THAT come across and buttoned and a bow on the tie. That's Baby Dolls! I just loved those shoes! My father used to buy them for me. And he would order these pretty dresses when I was small. I used to wear beautiful little dresses with a whole lotta lace to church, and they would have velvet bows an' a velvet band at the waist. Oh, boy! I thought I was dressed.

But when Rhoda and Molly came, I had got big—I was about nine—and that changed because we *all* wore the same thing—shoes, everything would be just alike—to school and to church. Peoples would say, "There go the three twins." My father say the reason why he dressed us like that because peoples couldn't say that Will put more on his daughter and better things on his daughter than he did his sister's children.

I remember the boy that I really loved named Jamie Watts. We'd go to Sunday school together. We'd call ourselves courting. We come up together from little. He lived over there not far from us. His mother was sick; she had T.B. Her husband had left her, and she had three boys, but Jamie's the one looked after his mother. He was small —we all were small—but he done all the cooking, all the washing and everything what his mother's sister didn't come and do. We'd be walking together to Sunday school, coming from Sunday school; and I would tote his hat—you see now what kinda courting—and he'd have my umbrella over me. Now wasn't that silly? He would carry that umbrella over me, and I would be carrying his hat! I really liked him, but I was too young.

So when we come home from church, my mother would

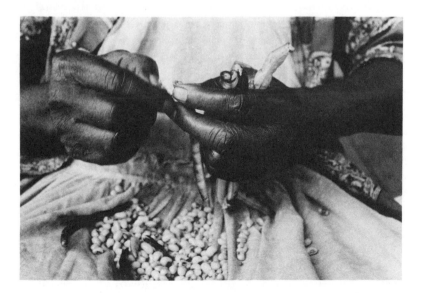

fix dinner—was macaroni and cheese and fried chicken or either chicken pie or dumplings and chicken and vegetables. We'd just eat until I'd go under the bed in the company room and go to sleep. And sometime after we would get through eating on Sunday, Jamie and his brothers —they lived over there not far from us—would come over to my father's house and we'd play church. We'd take our chairs outa our house and make a seat here and a row of seats over there. And someone make a table up there with boards and chairs. And we'd have a collection. We'd break up old plates, and that's the money. And we'd go to table; we'd be singing and strutting, going to the table. Go up and pay our money and come back.

Then somebody would preach. You know, we's acting as what they did at the church. Oh, I used to be a preacher! I used to *preach!* Get up there, and I'd be *"Hey,* hey man, and *glory* to *God* on *high!* Oh, *come* on *sisters* and *come* on and *give* me a *hand.* Ah *ha!* And *so* and *so* and *so!"* They'd come up shaking hands and "Hallelujah! Preach on!" Now that's what we did on Sunday evening.

WHEN I WAS SMALL, I USED TO TAKE CARE OF THE KIDS every day. My mother would be out working in the field around the house, and I would take them out in the yard, and we'd play in the dirt, and we'd make frog houses. You ever heard of frog houses? You dig a hole in the dirt, and you put your foot in there and pat it round your foot with your hand till it get firm, pull your foot out, and there would be a little house. Frogs would hop in it at night. Then we'd make mud cakes. Sometime if my mother and them was far enough off, I would take a piece of tin and two bricks and put that tin over them two bricks and make up a little fire under there, and that would be my stove. We'd steal meal or flour from the kitchen and cook pancakes and eat 'em. And I'd get up in the chinaberry tree lotta times, pick chinaberries, and make chains out of 'em for the kids with a thread and needle.

When I was about eight, I was nursing my sister Sallie. And I would put her to sleep, and instead a me going somewhere and sit down and play, I'd get my little old hoe and get out there and work right in the field around the house. I never was lazy; I always liked to work when I wasn't told. If you work when you're not told, you just don't have to go beyond it unlessen you want to. And then you get praise for it. But, oh boy! When I did have to go to work every day, I wished I was home.

So when we's old enough, we worked in the field. Sometime we'd work in somebody else's field, too, when we'd be caught up with our own. We used to hoe for Mr. Garret. And did you know we used to go up there and work for fifty cent a day? Hoe *all day long* for fifty cent! Sometime we'd turn that into syrup, a gallon of syrup to carry home. And if we did get out and work, my father didn't let us do like the kids do now. The kids go and do a little work, and their parents don't seed the money. But we worked; we didn't see it. My father did the collecting, 'cause he always provided for what we needed. So that's the way that went.

But July the Fourth, we'd have a big day because we'd be finished with our biggest work until time come then for us to pick cotton. We'd work half a day, and then we'd go downtown and buy us a block of ice and wrap it up in wool and carry it home in the wagon and bury it in the dirt

to keep it from melting so fast so we could make ice cream. And we'd have lemonade, and my mother would cook a cake and have chicken. It'd be good. That was the Fourth of July.

We laid the crop by in July, which meant you finish work in the field. And there wasn't much to do in August except pick peas and pull fodder. Revival would start in August. It'd just be different churches each week would call themself having a revival. They'd have a whole week preaching in the evening. They would be saving souls by peoples coming and joining the church, and then they'll baptize them at the end of the week. We would go from one church to the other'n during that revival time, because they'd have all of August for revivals waiting to pick the cotton.

We'd practically go every evening to *our* revival, because my father was a deacon. So we'd work in the daytime in the field and come home and wash up, and we'd get on that wagon and we'd get going to that meeting in the evening. The smaller children would sit up front with the older people so they wouldn't fall off, and the bigger children would sit on the board across the back. And if we didn't have the board to sit on across the back, we'd sit on the floor of the wagon with all our legs hanging out.

BY THE MIDDLE OF AUGUST, FIRST OF SEPTEMBER, THE cotton bolls'll start opening up, and then you start picking the cotton. I'd hate that cotton start to open; picking cotton was the tiredest thing! You had to stoop down all the time and pick it and put it in the sack hanging on your side. And then when you move, you gotta pull the sack. Then, when it get full, you have to go way over and put it in the basket and then come back. That stooping with the sack hung on your back, dragging up and down the row—oh, that was the most tiresome thing I ever seen.

So you empty the cotton in these baskets—my father used to make these baskets at night in the wintertime. Then you get on it and pack it, put in more and pack it, and you weigh it up. Rhoda picked 100 pounds by noon, and she probably picked 200 in a day. But I couldn't pick hardly

100 in a day. I would cheat when I go off to pick some cotton at other people's place. I'd pull off the green bolls and wrap it in the cotton. And cuckleburrs—them sticky balls that grow on a bush—I'd pull them off, even, and wrap it up in the cotton so it'd make it weigh. I *never* liked to pick cotton. I don't mind hoeing; to hoe in the field, I carried the head row. I was always ahead a everybody in the hoeing, 'cause I would hoe, and then, when I get my row out, I go back and help somebody else and get them out. But when it come to that cotton picking, I cheated, and I know I cheated. I was bad! Oh, trying to make a dollar.

BY THE TIME OCTOBER CAME, THAT'S THE TIME WE'D GO to school. We used to have to walk so long; we went through the woods and across little branches, you know, walking logs. We would run some and walk some.

When we was small and going to school, my father used to carry me over my lessons right after supper 'cause he was interested to see what I was learning. He used to go over my lessons with me all the time. I remember one night when I was learning my ABCs—I always was playful, and I never did take anything to heart, and the only way you could get me bound to studying anything was to give me a slap. When I was learning my ABCs, my father would tell me, "Go over those ABCs with me." He said, "What is this?" "*E.*" It'd be a *G* or maybe something else. I didn't know what it was because I would forget it no sooner'n he'd get through telling me what it was 'cause I just wasn't down at it, you know. He'd tell me, "If you wasn't so playful and listen to me, you would learn something." He'd tell me something, and if I come back over it the second time and didn't know it, he'd give me a slap. It'd upset me and I couldn't see then because I'd be crying; my eyes'd be fulla tears. He knew that if he didn't get down on me, I wouldn't do it. I could have learned a whole lot, but I didn't 'cause I didn't try. It's no fault of my father's, 'cause he was interested in me, but I didn't take much interest in myself. That was me.

When I was older, I was real fast. I used to *talk* fast and *walk* fast, and I *was* fast when I was coming up. I always had big legs, big at the top and come down little like a lamp chimney globe; they had shape and style! And we used to wear socks come up to your knee, and then they have this top that just folded over, and that top had little working around it. It was pretty. My father used to git 'em for us from Sears Roebuck. Sometime they be white or either they're blue with different kinda tops. They were beautiful. So I had big legs, which was popular in my days, and when I walked, I walked fast, and I popped my dress tail. Aunt Nina would say to her daughter, "Why don't you walk like Sara and pop your dress like her?" And I was always told I had a beautiful set a teeth; people would say, "Oh, say I do love to see you smile;" say, "You got the prettiest teeth." So I thought I was looking all right at that time, I guess.

But, anyway, I wasn't interested much in going to school. Instead of me learning what I was supposed to a been learning, I was always writing little notes to the one I later married. We'd be sending notes to and fro through school. When he's writing a note to me, he would say, "The road is wide, and I cannot step it. I love you, Baby; I cannot help it." And, "As the vine grow round the pine, Baby, I want you to be mine." I remember one time I was writing a letter, and I don't know where I got this from, but I had said on this letter, "Dear Jessie, I received your loving epistle today." And Professor Sanders got a chance to catch that note I was passing. He give me a good ole whipping that day about that. I used to be a *devil* when I was in school, and wouldn't we get a whipping with long switches! You stand out in front of 'im and swish, schwow! I wish he hadda kept on whipping me—I wouldn't a gotten married to this guy.

I always liked to be in every program that they had at school. We'd have a Thanksgiving program, a Christmas program, and a program at the end of school. I was in them because I could learn the poems and things that they telled me to learn. My father didn't have to hit me—not one time—when I was learning those poems, because that was something I wanted to do. And I could *act.* I could act in different plays that other kids was so bashful and couldn't learn things that I could learn. So anything that they wanted to learn at school and wanted to come out pretty good, they'd give it to me.

Oh, we'd have good plays. Professor Sanders would even invite white peoples. They would be sitting on the front rows. But one time I recited a poem, and I don't think my parents liked it. What was that now?

I've done stayed silent long enough,
An' tried to hold my breath,
But I must say a word or so
About these Jim Crow laws.
God made us all from white to black,
An' made us in one mold.
An' then He breathed us all to life
The breath that made the soul.
He gave us just one kind of day
An' just one kind of night;
An' that's enough to prove to all
This Jim Crow law ain't right.

Then it says:

We milk the cows;
We strain the milk;
We cook their cakes and pies.
One hand mix up the bread they eat,
An' that is no surprise.
We take their babies in our arms;
We hug and kiss and bite.
They make us face the Jim Crow law
An' tell me that it's right.
An' when some big thing come to town,
They'll put us in the back;
An' on the train we'll ride ahead
To catch what's on the track.
They'll mix us up with baggage, too,
An' everything in sight,
An' make us pay first-class fare,
An' pretend that that is right.
But to prove yourself a man

Is to vote an' judge the law,
An' come along this world can see
This Jim Crow law ain't right.

So they would give me poems like this to recite before an audience, and my father and mother would be there; they would come and listen. They cared, you know what I mean?

I was about twelve years old when my grandmother died. She was old, and she had got to where she went to wandering away from home, and she'd get lost. If somebody'd going to die, the death owl come to the house and cries "Ha, ha, ha, ha, ha, ha, ha, ha." And they'd say

that it was a sign of death. So you tie a knot in your sheet and say that would choke 'em and he won't quiver. All them old signs; they don't pay them things no attention no more. But whenever this owl be shivering, my momma's going to tie a knot in the sheet. She'd choke it so he'd stop saying that. The night before my grandmother died, this owl came up on the porch and was shivering. Sure did. Nobody couldn't sleep for that bird. So she did die.

My grandmother died about nine o'clock one morning, and one of my sisters, Essie, was born about eight o'clock that same morning in that same house. I ain't never been there when the baby was born; we always stayed at my mother's sister's house. They wouldn't tell us where the baby come from. They would tell us that the baby came from over behind the Blue Mountain or that the baby came out of a stump.

They let us go to Aunt Nina's to spend the night. When we come back the next morning, this baby was there, and Grandma died a little after that. It was time for breakfast. We went in the dining room, and when we come back in the house Aunt Ruth says, "Well, Momma slipped away from us while we was in the kitchen." My mother was in the other room; the baby was born just a few minutes before. So one went out, and one came in that same day.

THREE
Kitteneye

VERNA MAE SLONE

AS SHE RAISED UP, A PAIN struck her in the back and moved on around in front, down low. She clasped her hands against her body and said, "Oh, no, it can't be that; the baby han't due till April or the first of May. Jest an upset stomach; we've been eating too much of the same thing."

As she lifted the heavy latch to open the door, she saw a long hickory stick leaning against the side of the house. Nick had cut that the other day for ElCaney to ride as a horse. She took the hickory stick in one hand and the bucket in the other, and using the "horse" as a cane, she braced herself against the wind and started to the spring.

A thin sheet of ice had frozen over the top of the spring. She took her stick and tapped lightly on the ice and dipped her bucket in. Turning, she hurried back up the path. She saw that she had forgotten to close the door behind her after she had come out. As she set the bucket of water down on the side of the table, another pain hit her, much harder than the first. And as she grasped the edge of the table for support, she knew she had been fooling herself. It was her time, and the baby was saying, "Here I come, ready or not."

She filled the iron teakettle with water and set it before the fire, off to one side. Here it would soon be warm and out of her way, so she could bake some bread. She thought, "I will need all the strength I

28

can muster, so I won't take time to fix a plum out-and-out
mess; I will just make a snack for me and ElCaney."

The thought never entered her mind to be afraid; it was
just something that had to be done. "Women were made
to bear children; children, the Good Book had said . . . in
pain you shall bear them." Of course she did not enjoy
pain, but it was something to be gotten over with. She tried
to keep her mind on the great joy she would have when it
was over.

It wasn't long before ElCaney woke up. "Oh, Maw, I
smell hotcakes and meat, and I shore am hungry."

"Well, jump up, son, and eat. Don't mind putting your
shoes on, fer soon as you eat, you have to go back to
bed."

"Oh, Maw!"

"You know I mean what I say and I say what I mean."

After they had eaten, she made ElCaney go back to bed.

"Turn ye face toward the wall and don't look around till
I tell ye," said Frankie.

"But, Maw, why?"

"Do as I say and no 'why' to it." She wished Caney
wasn't here; he was too young.

"You know I told you how the ole hoot owl was going
to bring us another little un."

Another pain came so hard and sharp that she sank to
the floor, caught her breath, and murmured, "Please God,
let me keep my mind, so I can take care of this little un
You're sending me." She realized the baby was being born.
She could not even get to the bed, and pulling Caney's
pallet before the fire, she braced herself for the coming of
her child.

In less than an hour, Caney, still facing the wall, heard a
small, weak cry almost like a kitten, and he said, "Can I
look now, Maw?"

"Now listen, Caney, and listen good. Ye take that
hickory stick Nick cut fer ye a hoss and knock down some
of them wearing thangs on that pole, and ye bring me my
underskirt, that white un, and bring me some twine from
that wood box under the bed. And reach me the knife
from the table."

"Shore, Maw."

"And hurry, son."

And Caney scrambled from the bed, feeling very important as he got all the things his maw had asked for. Still hearing the small whimpering voice, he could not believe it was a baby's, it was so low and weak.

It seemed to him like hours before his mother called him to her side and showed him what she had wrapped in her white underskirt. And when he looked, he almost gasped.

"But, Maw, it's so puny."

"Yeah, under three pounds is my guess, but ye know he has this whole big world to grow in. He is almost as small as a kitten."

And ElCaney answered, "Kitten, Maw! Why he han't as big as a kitten's eye."

And that, my dear grandchildren, is how my father became known as Kitteneye. Although the name written in the Good Book was Isom B. Slone, he was to be stuck with the name Kitteneye all his born days.

FOUR

Born for Hard Luck

ALLEN TULLOS

ARTHUR "PEG LEG SAM" *Jackson was born near Jonesville, South Carolina, about 25 miles southeast of Spartanburg, on December 18, 1911. When only a child he was put to plowing by his father and often hired-out for extra work to neighbors. Young Arthur, however, took a fancy to playing the harmonica and riding freight trains. One longtime Jonesville resident remembers that Arthur, upon hearing an approaching train, once left his mule harnessed in the field and ran for the railroad tracks. He was gone for months.*

Peg first joined the medicine show circuit in 1938. For years, Peg acted as straightman for various funnymen whose routines of eclectic patter were a hodge-podge of folk humor, minstrel remnants and slapstick buffoonery. The shows were designed to draw crowds of farm and mill families, who might buy snake oil or curative soaps.

Peg's stories of hoboing and wandering, odd-jobbing, playing harmonica and passing the hat on street corners, reconstruct the plights of countless creative, restless Southern black men who could find few satisfactory outlets for their energies in the long years of Jim Crow culture. Scarred and battered, yet exuberant, Peg has somehow survived. He recounts in fascinating episodic fashion a life lived by wits and endurance, offering insights and visions as well as prejudices and illusions. **31**

THE FIRST TIME I CAUGHT A FREIGHT TRAIN I WAS TEN
years old. Rode it from Spartanburg to Columbia, South
Carolina. Just warming up, getting used to it. Then I run
away again, down to Lockhart. They hid me in a mill. I
worked for them three days, till I was about dead—too
young for that job.

And my mother came down there to get me. "You seen
a little boy that can dance so?" They said, "Yeah, he works
back there rollin cotton to be packed." She hid and they
called for me. I come out there and they said, "Let's see
you dance one time." I cut a few steps and Ma run out
and grabbed me. Back home we came on a train. The
conductor like to have preached me to death. "Why don't
you stay at home, son?" I thought to myself, "God, I wish I
could get off this train." I reckon I stayed at home three
days—gone again. Yeah, I was gone again.

Next time I took a trip from Spartanburg to Charleston,
laid around down there awhile, then I decided I'd go
further. I caught the Southern to Asheville, then into
Virginia. Mother couldn't find me then, I was too long
gone. I went on up into Ohio, caught the C. & O. Then I
came back home again and stayed about a week. Plow
time, I didn't like to plow. Picking cotton time, I said, "Uh
oh, got to go again."

I left out that time and landed in Indianapolis, Indiana.
Gettin further then, gettin trained-up good. I was about
twelve years old then. I laid around there awhile, eating out
of garbage cans and eating out of farmers' fields. I never
hurt the farmer bad. I'd get a dozen roasting ears and build
a big fire at night. I'd throw the ears in there shuck and all.
The steam from the shuck would cook it. Boy, you talk
about some mouth-smacking food. I'd sit back and eat a
dozen at a time. Sometime I'd go up and get me another
dozen to carry with me.

Kept a little sack on my back with a blanket in it, maybe
a pair of overalls in it. If anybody washed, I'd get me a
pair. Country people used to wash down by the spring and
hang them out, I'd look for that all the time. I'd go by, pull
off my dirty pair and carry away the clean pair.

I RODE MORE FREIGHT TRAINS THAN DAYS I GOT TO LIVE.
All around through Florida, Alabama, Georgia, Louisiana,
Texas. What got away with me one time was that Southern
Pacific. I caught it out of Louisiana one night—they called it
the Sunset Limited. And it never did stop for nothing out
through the sandy desert. I was hungry, my God! Stomach
thought my throat was cut. When it got to Los Angeles, the
first garbage can I seen, I rushed to it, heels went over my
head.

I know every hobo jungle. From Alexandria, Virginia—
with the ice cars. We'd drink rubbing alcohol there.
Sometime we'd kill a pig or a cow. Four or five of us
would carry him back and boy we had a ball that night.
Hoboes telling lies and I was in there with em. Up there in
Toledo, Ohio—the biggest hobo convention in the world.
We had a sign hanging up, "When you eat, wash the pan
and hang it up again. Another hobo, our friend, may come
in."

Oh, I had a good living. Didn't have no home, always
followed the season. I'd go down in Florida when it got
cold, sleep outdoors. I slept outdoors half my life.

When I had two good feet I could catch the trains
making forty miles an hour. When I lost my foot, I'd catch
them making twenty-five miles an hour. I hoboed more
after I got it cut off. Never caught the front car, always
caught the back car so it would whup me up behind it.

I lost my leg in Raleigh. I was coming out of Richmond. I
had gone uptown and bummed some of those ends they
cut off meat. I got me some ends and come on back down
near the tracks and laid down, I was right tired. My buddy
shook me and said, "Train coming." That's all I remember.
I caught it but I don't know how I fell off. I believe my
head bumped under that bridge. You seen them things
hanging down at bridges? That's to warn you before you
get to it. I believe that bridge was too low for a man on
top. I believe I caught it that way, half asleep when I
caught it.

When I found myself, I was laying down on the rails. I
thought, "My old leg done gone to sleep." And I got up,
looked down, and my shoe was cut off my foot. Shoe split
wide open. I said, "Mhnn, mhnn." Never felt bad till then.

I fell back down on the railroad and yonder come the yard master. "Hoboing was you?" I says, "Sho was." "Let me see what I can do for you." He called the ambulance. About that time about a thousand people were up on the bridge looking down on me. They lifted me out of there and carried me to St. Agnes Hospital. They might be done changed the name now. That's been about forty-six years ago.

I stayed in the hospital a month and a half. That leg didn't start hurtin until a week after they done took it off. They didn't have the stuff they got now to stop pain. That thing throbbin for three weeks. After that got good, another fellow come in there with his leg cut off, like to bled to death. I give him a quart of blood. They said, "We're gonna give you a big meal if you give him some blood." I was greedy to eat and wasn't used to nothing but a garbage can. I give him that. I give him that blood and they give me a big plate. I like to ate myself to death. When I got out of there, I had $2.02 when I got off at Spartanburg, coming home, and crutches—they gave me a pair of crutches. I stayed at home about a year after that, then took off again.

**Arthur
"Peg Leg Sam"
Jackson**

*You look at me, you look at a man that was born for
    hard luck.*
I was born on the thirteenth day, on Friday, bad luck day.
I was born the last month in the year.
I was born the last week in the month.
I was born the last day in the week.
I was born the last hour in the day.
I was born the last minute in the hour.
I was born the last second of the minute.
I come near not gettin here at all.

To show you that I am in hard luck,
If I go up the street walking fast, I run over something.
If I go up there walking slow, something runs over me.
*I'm in such hard luck, if I'm sitting down, I'm in
    everybody's way.*
*I'm in such hard luck that if it's raining down soup at
    this very minute,*
*Everybody would be standing there with a spoon, why,
    I'd have a fork.*
I'm in such hard luck that if my daddy was to die,
They'd make a mistake and bury me.
I'm in such hard luck,
If I was to die they'd make me walk to the cemetery.
I was born for hard luck.

FIVE

Scientific Methodology

WILL D. CAMPBELL

FOR YEARS WE HAD A place at school called "down the hill." It was a grove of trees a few hundred yards behind the schoolhouse where we went at recess time for toilet purposes. There were no plumbing facilities in the building and not even an outhouse nearby. So we used the woods, each little clique having their own favorite place which the members would use and guard with fervor and dedication against any who dared threaten their territorial rights. But a W.P.A. project had recently built a "facility" for our use and we were told never to relieve ourselves outside that structure again because, it was carefully explained, such a practice led to the spread of the dread hookworms.

We saw this as oppressive in itself, but the day a technician from the State Health Department visited the school with a program to detect who among us already had hookworms we were morally outraged.

First the man explained that he was operating with a grant from Washington. This, we supposed, was to indicate the magnitude of what he was about to say. He said the purpose of the grant was to rid our community of hookworms, adding that the South was backward, not so much because of the Civil War, but because of malaria and hookworms. (We had not known until then that we were backward and therefore had not pondered the possible reasons for our backwardness.) He passed out a mimeographed, one-sheet set of instructions, rolled around a small tin can looking then like a snuff can and looking now like a container for filmstrips. Total silence was required for five minutes while we read what it was we were expected to do.

"Are there any questions?"

There were no immediate questions because no one understood enough of what he had read to evoke a question.

Now the principal spoke. "Now if any of you have any questions you had better ask them now because every last one of these specimen cans must be returned tomorrow."

This did elicit a question and one of the high school boys asked it for all of us.

"What is a specimen?"

"A specimen is. . . ." The principal glared at the visitor who appeared relieved that the question was not directed at him. Mr. Stuart continued.

"A specimen is . . . a specimen is a small amount of something."

Now we knew how much but we didn't yet know how much of what. The instruction sheet had said to place a specimen of feces in the container, write our full name and the names of both our parents on the label, and return it to school the following day. But "feces" was no more a word of our vocabulary than "specimen."

Gradually it began to dawn on us in the form of a very vague notion that the entire operation had to do with what we called "taking a crap." But it had not yet come into clear focus for any of us. And did not during the whispering and mumbling that was going on throughout the hall, not until one of the smaller boys, thinking that he was speaking softly enough so that he would not be heard by anyone except himself, said, "I know. He's telling us to go home and shit in a snuff can."

What he said was heard by those immediately surrounding him. They in turn shared it with others and in not more than a minute howls and uncontrollable laughter had spread over the auditorium like the fires that came to the Moore Pasture in early spring.

The embarrassed representative of the Health Department stood glowering at the principal, arms folded tightly across his chest. The rage of the principal was so obvious to us that the noise subsided as quickly as it had begun. Now the hall was a sea of compelled silence, all the boys sitting with teeth clenched, lips drawn tightly together to hold the thundering mirth churning and tearing at our insides, bellies almost bursting from our efforts to control muscles which would not be controlled. And when the principal, seeing that the tortuous restraint would not hold for long, said, "That's all," every voice exploded and there was pandemonium. School was out.

Now we were far back in the Moore Pasture woods, laughed out, not finding any of it funny anymore.

All of us resented the idea that the government had the right to know what our "feces" looked like. And we found no humor in this demeaning act of having to bring ourselves to such close contact with our body waste. Still we knew that it must be done.

But Joe, lagging behind the rest of us, reading again the instruction sheet, found a means of protest.

"It says, 'place a specimen of feces' in the container. It doesn't say, 'Place a specimen of *your* feces' in the container." The creative dissenter was right. Of course! One boy could provide the specimen for us all.

But which one? Joe said since it was his idea he should be excepted and asked for a volunteer, looking straight at me in a manner that told me I should not offer. When no one volunteered he suggested that we say, "Eeny, meeny, miney, moe. Catch a nigger by the toe. If he hollers, make him pay, fifty dollars every day." Joe had earlier shared with me the method he had of making that come out wherever he wanted it to. There were many combinations, but by first counting the number of persons and starting the rhyme with the person on his immediate left, he knew in advance which one would be chosen.

As is so often the case with social protest and community organizing there was a problem we had not reckoned with. When the laboratory report was returned we learned that our common donor *had* hookworms, meaning we *all* had hookworms and all of us were required to undergo the treatment or confess to our misdeed. We chose to swallow the pills, big pills, almost the size of bird eggs.

Joe, who was later to become a scientist himself, raised a question about the scientific method which had not occurred to me. He wondered why the researcher did not find it strange that while *all* the Campbell boys had hookworms, not *one* Campbell girl was found to be similarly infested.

SIX

Working Late at the Club

WEKESA MADZIMOYO

WHEN I WAS FIFTEEN, MY mother moved back home to Fayetteville, North Carolina, from New York. In need of cash, she pawned a Polaroid camera. A few weeks later, my father helped me get the camera out of pawn, and I became pretty good with the Polaroid 103.

Around the corner from my house was a club called the Savoy Supper Club. My father would go to that club from time to time. And after seeing some folk there taking and selling photographs, one day he suggested that I go to the club to sell pictures. I said, reluctantly, "Well." He said, "Well, why don't you then!?" He urged me on, bought the necessary film and flashbulbs, and talked to the owner of the place.

When he first took me out there, I was nervous, to say the least. I had never been in the club at night and was too young to pay and enter at the door if I had wanted to. Dad would sit back and observe me for a while; then he'd call me over and say, "Listen, you ought to move around more, ask more people—greet them and tell them what you have to offer." He'd then sit back again and watch to make sure no one was "clipping" or "messing" with his son. I got the hang of it in spite of the threats like, "Give me your money or I'll whip your ass," or open homosexual advances like, "When are you gonna let me pluck you?"

I was scared, but it was

challenging and exciting. It was also a way for me to earn
some money. I was able to help my mother buy toys and
other things for my younger sisters; I bought my own
clothes and a car while still in high school.

I worked that job until I left to go to college. By that
time, the business had grown; I had contracted with three
clubs and hired photographers to work in each. I traded
cameras about every three months at one of the many
local pawn shops. I'd pay fifteen or twenty dollars with my
trade-in for another model.

I traded them in 'cause using them every week would
wear them out. Night club business in 1969 was really fine.
So good that the brother-owner closed the Savoy and
opened up a bigger joint. However, with the move came
competition. The owner decided to allow someone else to
take photographs. When I confronted the owner, he said,
"Well, both of you do it." I said "All right," but I knew
that it would mean a cut in profit. I was angry and
depressed. Again, my father came to my aid: "Don't
worry. Just go out and do a better job."

Knowing that my photos were better, I would
photograph couples that the other guy already
photographed—free of charge, so they could compare. I
began offering guarantees, discounts on volume, free
photos. I was also a young kid "hustling to make it." Black

folk liked seeing a young black kid trying to make an honest dollar. After three weeks of doing battle, my competition left.

But working at the club was not all fun and games. I also had to deal with Afrikan-Americans who had adopted as their model the values and appearances of white folk. "Make me light, now," they would say. I was pleased that there were other Afrikan-Americans who, being proud of their Afrikanness and ebony complexion, would be dissatisfied if the picture showed them lighter than they really were.

I learned to deal with folk who were angry or stoned and didn't want to pay for their pictures. One fellow even threatened to shoot me 'cause a photograph "didn't look like his wife." This was no idle threat. The man went to his car to get his pistol. Immediately, I borrowed a gun from a friend inside the club. And while talking to his wife about the photos, I "accidentally" brushed open my coat, displaying my borrowed gun. A few minutes later, when her husband returned, she convinced him that a fight over the picture wasn't worth the trouble. To say that I was relieved was an understatement. I had never fired a gun in my life!

On balance, the years at the club were great. During this time, I was developing my political ideas about oppression, liberation, and racism; I was writing about my frustrations at King's being killed, reading Malcolm, and helping to organize the Black Student Union at Terry Sanford Senior High. Through the club, I was in touch in another way with poor black people. What I saw there was some of the beauty and ugliness of my people, which enabled me to see better some of the ugliness and beauty in myself. And all of this happened around the corner from my house.

SEVEN
Portraits

ROBERT COOPER
AND THE CHILDREN
OF BRAXTON
COUNTY SCHOOLS

THE PHOTOGRAPHS
that follow resulted from the
Artists-in-the-Schools program
in Braxton County, West
Virginia. They were made by
public school students ten to
fourteen years old.

This is a wonderful age to
begin taking pictures.
Photography offers kids a
chance to frame experience—
that is, to hold it apart for
special consideration, and then
to "frame" it again in an
exhibit or magazine to be
considered by others. The
medium is personal, nonverbal,
and widely accessible. Many
students who are hesitant in
speaking and writing are
immediately successful at
self-expression with a camera.

I encouraged the students to
respond to familiar subjects and
to work with feelings. Their
ability to tap these sources
enables many students to
transcend the limits of simple
cameras or the lack of refined
technique. Photography is first
of all a process of
understanding what one sees.
Walker Evans says of the
camera, "You have to really
know something before you
dare point it." These young
photographers in Braxton
County automatically have two
things professional
artist-photographers are always
striving for: intimate access to
powerful subject matter and a
fresh point of view. The camera
offers kids a chance to trace
personal experience in an
instant.

Although much that
happens in student

43

photographs can be termed accidental, I believe much more of it is intuitive. Through photographs, kids are easily able to show us what they care most about. (This became easier still for our younger students when they switched to Polaroid.)

As editor of the student work, I felt it was important to remain true to the simple moods of quiet contemplation and youthful exuberance the students enjoyed while actually working with their cameras. I tried not to present the photographs in a manner the workers had not intended for their product. Photography (and editing) has tremendous potential for misuse and for exploitation of the subject. The camera can make almost anything appear foolish and unimportant; but these are all positive images, sympathetically observed, presented for our appreciation.

Many years have passed since I sat in the same classrooms. Because I had been here before, the project held a special magic for me that it would have held in no other place. I believe in this place, and I believe in these kids partly because I see in each of them potential, see myself at an earlier time. By offering them photography, I offered them my means of seeing and dealing with a special world we have in common, and I fulfilled a promise to the ten-year-old kid I once was.

ABOVE: Untitled Photograph by Sarah Miller

LEFT: "Bus Driver, Dallas Delaney" by Doug Ramsey

46

ABOVE: Untitled Photograph by Lena Smith

BELOW: "Pierre" by Richard Bender

ABOVE: "My Sister Donna" by Janet Wimer

BELOW: "My Grandmother" by Paul Conrad

ABOVE: "Dining Room of My Grandparents' House" by
Candy Wine

BELOW: "Mrs. Greene" by Robert Goldsmith

ABOVE: "Self-Portrait with Younger Sister" by Laura
Carroll

BELOW: "Dumpling Run" by Terry Van Kirk

ABOVE:
Untitled
Photograph by
Joe Litton

RIGHT:
"Self-Portrait"
by Mary
Jenkins

Interlude

Bachlor Uncle, a Photograph
DWIGHT CHILDERS

Vernon's eyes kindle still.

The others said only:
"Vernon never married:
he was very serious-minded and
never took any interest in the girls.
He always dressed up fine,
even for picnics.
Nobody could say a prettier prayer.
He was made a deacon very young."

But Uncle, I know.
You gave me my own gifts.
Once, with you beside,
I saw myself in a still creek pool.
You laughed, blew ripples,
then let me look again.
(Next birthday you gave me a polished agate
plucked from that creek side.)

Once, when time was ripe
you told me the history of passion:
Calvin, of the Harley-Davidson
across Soco and on into Georgia:
Daniel, poet who died young in Georgia:
Andrew, who never came back from Normandy.
These were not secrets, but air and water.

Now, dear Vernon, I have you
to thank for almost everything.

To the Office
JOYCE GREEN, GRADE 7

I remember when Miss Smith sent me to the office because she told me to go sit down and I started to dance and she carried me to the office. She made me so sick I can kill her with her flat rear end. She made Mr. Jones take my pecans, and I haven't got them back yet. Miss Smith told Mr. Jones I was dancing in the room and called her a name and that's a story. When I got back she thought sure I had got a whipping. Miss Smith told me if I didn't stop talking I was going back to the office. I told her I was not thinking about her.

A World by Myself
ANTONIO WALKER, GRADE 6

When I be looking out the window at the rain
It seem like I am deaf
It seem like I am in a new world
And I don't know anyone then.
When I be doing my work in class
I look at a word so hard
I be in a world by myself.

EIGHT

Wonder and Glory in Another Century

LARRY GOODWYN

MY CHILDHOOD memories of Virginia don't seem to count. Some formative process doubtless was at work, but it was soft and effortless, as in a cocoon. The only thing about the years in Virginia that comes to mind is that my father, an army officer, always disagreed with other army officers about two things. The first was about Roosevelt. My father loved Franklin Roosevelt. The second was that in the next war America wasn't going to fight the Bolshevik Russians. The U.S. Army officer corps was pretty serious about fighting the Bolsheviks. But my father said we were going to fight the Fascists—Germany, Italy, and Japan.

One or the other of these two topics, the New Deal and the coming war, was usually the center of discussion at dinner all through our Virginia years in the early 1930s. Not that I grasped these matters with great subtlety. For me personally, the first fragile awakening of self into the surrounding world of one's provincial origins did not come in Virginia; it came when we moved to Texas in 1936. At the age of eight, I discovered football, Texas-style.

The first thing I learned about those Texans was that they liked crowds. Many years later, as an editor of the *Texas Observer,* I would realize that the crowds were mere effect, a manifestation of a much more organic tribal folkway that was central to the very

53

Youth Rodeo in Central Texas

way of life of the state. Football was no mere two- or three-hour pageant on an autumn weekend; it was an instrument of psychic survival and, as such, a centerpiece of the regional culture.

In places like Brownwood and Odessa and Big Springs, and even in small places like Olney and Rockdale and Sonora, the Friday night high school football game was a civic celebration, a rite of passage not merely for the male teenagers on the field or the female cheerleaders on the sidelines but for the whole society. Towns of five thousand population had football stadiums that seated six thousand and regularly bulged with seven thousand. Middle-aged parents, men and women in western shirts and blue jeans, helped Grandpa and Grandma up the steps to the thirtieth row, the barefooted kids running ahead, the last-born in

Mama's arms or hanging tightly to her hand. The mayor was there and the town banker and the local wildcatter, indistinguishable in their Stetsons and boots from the clerks and ranchers and roughnecks who worked for them or were mortgaged to them.

In the eastern part of the state—the piney woods—the cast and the power relationships were the same, though the ranchers there were mostly farmers. In the east, though, the ritual was a little less intense, a little less transcendent, for there were other things to do sometimes. Friday night at the high school stadium was still the high point, but it wasn't everything. Fishing and hunting in the creeks and pine forests offered additional varieties of ritual.

But in west Texas—in the world of the Great Plains beyond the Edwards Plateau—the streams and forests had shriveled into dry arroyos and trackless land marked only with scrawny mesquites. In this stark country, the wind blew endlessly and the sand beat against clapboard, sifted under the sills and into the furniture and even into the food. Mostly, the sand and the wind beat against the people and into their skin pores, a silent unseen intimidation that produced leathery faces and a fear in the soul. The plains wind haunted the women, gnawed at the men, as if to insist endlessly that they had no business being there, that this was the land of the Comanche if it belonged to any humans at all.

You had to move through this world slowly, live in it awhile, to know that the loud shouts and rowdiness of the people were more than some kind of peculiar regional heartiness. At root, it was a desperate defense, a fragile assertion of hope and defiance against the plains wind and the searing, dry summers and the dry, raw cold of the winters. Here, football had become the collective defense, the celebration of community, a ritual proclamation not only that "We are here!" but that "We are prevailing!" In Plano and Rawls, in Jackboro and Montague, the Friday night game and the astonishing pageantry that surrounded it represented a tribal assertion that the people were winning their struggle against the land and the wind.

I KNEW NONE OF THIS IN 1936 WHEN THE FAMILY CAME TO
Texas, the soft rhythms of Virginia still informing my ways
of thinking. But the attempt at socialization, the effort to
turn Southerners into Texans, began, I now understand,
right away. In the very first year, the Austin Maroons
became a principal focus of my leisure. The tailback had
the marvelous name of Travis Raven. (Ah, the names were
regional statements: Kyle Rote and Yale Lary and Chal
Daniel and Doak Walker—names for *football* players.)

It needs to be said at the outset that there is not too
much wonder associated with the Austin Maroons. Glory,
yes, but not wonder. The Austin Maroons were already at
the top when I found them in 1936—at the absolute top,
like second-generation robber barons. When Travis Raven
graduated and went off to college, somebody found a boy
out in the countryside who was big and strong and fast.
Somebody else gave his daddy, a tenant farmer, a job in
Austin, and the boy moved into Travis Raven's slot at
tailback. A fitting anonymity surrounded all this: the new
star was named Jones. The Austin Maroons clobbered
everybody with Raven, and they clobbered everybody with
Jones. For years, they ruled effortlessly as champions of
District 15-AA. Glory, but not wonder.

Horatio Alger lived on the other side of town—at the
University of Texas.

Friends and neighbors, we started in rags. Winless.
Absolutely winless. The forces of the culture beat down on
us poor folks. SMU and TCU and Rice and Baylor all
manhandled the state university. The Eyes of Texas weren't
on anybody. We looked at the ground in front of us, heads
bowed in weekly humiliation. You people at Notre Dame
and USC and Michigan don't know how it was, in poverty.
Let me tell you, it was diminishing. It made you feel poorly.
It made you edgy. You got laughed at and people
patronized you. It wasn't nothin' to be a Longhorn.

The story really begins in late November 1936, the last
game of the year. Thanksgiving Day. The Traditional Game
against the "other" state university, the Aggies of Texas
A&M. It is very important that you understand about "the
Tradition." The Tradition was that the Aggies had never
won in Austin. Not since Memorial Stadium was built and

dedicated, in a game against the Aggies, way back in 1924. Now then, when you are eight years old, that is some Tradition. The Aggies never won in Austin. Never!

But they sure were favored in 1936, because, as everybody knew, the Longhorns couldn't beat *anybody.*

Well, they did this time. I was there that day when old Tradition just kept rolling along. Kern Tips of the Humble Radio Network said it just right: "When the long November shadows lengthened across Memorial Stadium, the scoreboard read Texas 7, Texas A&M 0." That's the way Kern Tips usually talked.

You know, of course, that the way up from rags isn't all that easy. There were still plenty of hard times ahead. The Longhorns couldn't win anything all through 1937. Nine straight defeats, culminating on Thanksgiving Day in Aggieland. Still on the bottom.

A float made of paper flowers said it best, in the spring Roundup Parade on the campus in 1938. I saw it. It had a Bible made of black paper flowers and a brown flower football and a student standing between them in a football uniform. On the side of the float were the words, "The Answer to Our Prayers."

The answer, you see, was Dana X. Bible, the famous football coach, who had been lured away from Nebraska to bring the University of Texas out of the wilderness. There was a lot of talk about it because they gave him a ten-year contract at $15,000 per year and a lifetime contract as athletic director after that at $5,000 per year. In the Depression, they did this. The only problem was that the president of the university didn't make that much, so they raised him, too.

Boy, it was like a lightning bolt. Ole Dana Bible stirred up the alumni (they were pretty stirred up going in), and Bible and everybody else combed Texas, and let me tell you, they got some football players in there in 1938. That freshman team made everybody sit up and take notice. They had a big guy at fullback named Pete Layden and a tricky little guy at tailback named Jack Crain, and they had a rangy end named Malcolm Kutner, and they just beat up on folks. Everybody just couldn't wait until 1939, when those freshmen would be eligible to play varsity football.

Especially after what happened to the varsity in that year of 1938. It was terrible—they just kept right on losing. Every week. As September turned into October and then into November, that victory over the Aggies in 1936 was all we could look back on. We hadn't won a game in two years!

THE SOUTHWEST CONFERENCE WAS REAL BIG IN THOSE days, of course. Everybody in America knew that. When unbeaten SMU played TCU, the winner got to go to the Rose Bowl and the loser went to the Sugar Bowl. Slinging Sammy Baugh and his TCU team lost, but you can bet they won that Sugar Bowl game. And then in 1938, TCU had another great passer, Davey O'Brien, and all he did was take 'em to the National Championship. The Southwest Conference was the best there was. Everybody knew that.

You also have to understand that there is a real villain here. His name is Harry Viner, and his part of the story started in 1937 when Rice Institute came to town. Texas had it won late in the game when this Rice guy threw a long pass that bounced in the end zone and then into the hands of a Rice player named Frank Steen. It was incomplete—the ball *bounced* on the ground just before this guy Steen picked it up. But the referee ruled it complete! The referee was Harry Viner. They almost had a riot that afternoon. The papers next day called the Rice end "One Bounce" Steen. But that wasn't anything compared to what everybody called Viner. We'd have won a game in 1937 if it hadn't been for Harry Viner.

That was how things stood on Thanksgiving Day in 1938. We were worried. Burt Newlove, who lived next door to me, said there wasn't any way Texas could win, 'cause the Aggies had a real good team, not quite as good as TCU, the national champions, but right up there. Rexito Hopper and his brother, Jackie, were like me. They were hoping. But Garland Smith was with Burt. Garland said that old Tradition was going down for sure this time. Course, they hoped it wouldn't, you understand. We *all* were for the Longhorns. That was like being for Roosevelt. It was just too bad those marvelous freshmen that Dana Bible had couldn't play. We really needed them.

HERE'S WHAT HAPPENED. BURT AND REXITO AND I WERE IN the twenty-five-cent Knot Hole Gang section, in the end zone, and saw it all. That stadium was packed. Forty thousand people. And Texas played inspired football. They drove down to the Aggie five-yard line. They drove down to the eight. They drove down to the six.

But they couldn't score.

Once, after Texas had been stopped short on fourth down, somebody said they should have tried to kick a field goal. But that didn't make any sense at all, because everybody knew that Texas couldn't even kick an extra point, let alone a field goal.

Anyway, in the second half, Texas was just as inspired. The Longhorns stopped the Aggies cold, but they still couldn't manage to score. One of the troubles was the reverse to Puett. We had this player in the backfield named Puett. He only carried the ball on a reverse, which was not often. Most times he didn't even get back to the line of scrimmage. They'd just see that old reverse coming, and they would clobber poor Puett. Especially on fourth down around the Aggie goal line. Well, late in the game, we made one last drive down to their ten-yard line. The fullback made two. Then the tailback made five. I remember it exactly. I felt pretty good because we were down on the three-yard line, and we had two more plays to buck it over. One to get it right down to the goal line and another one to buck it right on over. I remember thinking that, while standing there (believe me, we were all standing!) in the Knot Hole Gang section in the end zone.

You know what happened? On third down, they gave the ball to Puett on a reverse. He started to swing outside like he always did, but then he cut right upfield. I could see the hole. From the end zone, you can see holes easy, even when the teams are at the other end of the field. When he got to the line of scrimmage, he just dove. High. He was three feet in the air, his body all strung out parallel to the ground. Touchdown! There's a newspaper picture of that, Puett soaring high with that Aggie goal line right under him! It was in every paper in Texas next day.

And they kicked the extra point, too! It just went right on up there, not exactly "splitting the uprights" like they say, but almost, and it was way up there, not just barely getting over the crossbar or anything like that. Texas 7, Aggies 0. Old Burt Newlove and Rexito Hopper and I just went wild, jumping up and down. Everybody went wild. The Tradition was going to make it!

But it wasn't over. In fact, something really crazy and unbelievable happened.

With about a minute to go, Texas had the ball at midfield and the punter aimed the ball for the coffin corner and hit it. It bounced just inside the sideline at the one-yard line and went straight on out of bounds. Aggies on the one, with ninety-nine yards of Memorial Stadium Tradition looking them right square in the face. They were whipped! But you know what? The referee ruled that the ball had *not* gone out of bounds. He waved his hands and said it had gone in the end zone. Dana Bible had a fit. Players ran off the bench, and things got pretty hot where that referee was. That referee was Harry Viner!

There was a kind of scuffle—at least Harry Viner later claimed somebody pushed him—and he just marched that ball up to the twenty-yard line and he kept right on marching. Harry Viner penalized Texas half the distance to our goal line. Crazy! Half of eighty yards is forty yards! The place almost came apart. It must have been the longest penalty in the history of football.

But Texas stayed right in there. They rushed that Aggie passer off his feet and made him throw three wild, incomplete passes. The Aggies had to punt. The ball just hung up there lazily and came down and got killed on the Texas five-yard line. Less than thirty seconds to go.

Well, Dana Bible put ole Bobby Moers in there. He was an All-American, Bobby Moers was. But it was in basketball. He played guard. He was the greatest dribbler the Southwest Conference had ever had. And they put him in there at tailback and centered the ball to him.

Bobby dribbled it. On the ground. In the Texas end zone. And an Aggie fell on it! Can you believe that? In the Traditional Game. In Memorial Stadium. Where the Aggies have never won or tied even.

And so, of course, the Aggies kicked the extra point. *But it never got there.* The University of Texas blocked that

extra point on Thanksgiving Day in 1938 on the last play of
the Traditional Game. About four guys just poured in, and
one of them leaped up high on the backs of the others and
put both hands out, and that ball smashed into those two
hands and rocketed right back upfield, right past the kicker.

We couldn't kick an extra point, but on Thanksgiving
Day in 1938 we beat those Aggies 7–6 in Memorial
Stadium. "We only won one game all year, but those
Aggies haven't won in Memorial Stadium yet." It was
golden.

Nobody left, of course. It couldn't be allowed to end.
People just stayed. The Longhorn band played "The Eyes
of Texas," and Burt and Rexito and I squared our shoulders
and sang that song like we never sang it before. "All the
live long day." Yes sir! And walking home, across
Speedway Boulevard and across the campus and then up
the drag and over to Rio Grande Street and up to
Washington Square where we lived, visions swam in our
heads and our lips gave wings to poems. Puett on a
reverse. Puett on the Reverse for three yards, soaring into
history, high over that Aggie goal line. Did you see old
Puett fly, Rexito? Yeah, boy, I saw it! Boy, what a play!
Boy, what a Game!

Can life ever again approach such a moment of ecstasy?
Will there ever be a sight like that Texas line smothering
that extra point? On the last play of the Traditional Game?
Let TCU have the National Championship. We have the
greatest tradition in the world: the Aggies do not win in
Memorial Stadium.

And Harry Viner. A new tradition. Harry Viner does not
referee University of Texas football games ever again. The
end, Harry Viner. There is, in 1938, no question in our
minds that there is a just God and that the American
Republic is under the rule of law.

THAT WAS HOW IT STARTED. IT MARKED THE BEGINNING OF
all the magic still to come over the next three years. The
fabulous freshmen who could not play that day became the
sensational, erratic sophomores of 1939, the maturing
juniors of 1940, and what *Life* magazine called the

American "Wonder Team" of 1941. It was "the greatest college football team ever assembled." The Wonder Team simply crushed people. They beat the fifth-ranked team in the nation, SMU, 34–7. Rice went down 40–0 and Arkansas 48–14. The Oklahoma Sooners surrendered 40–7. The magnetic moments, so many of them, fuse in my memory into a luminous hue, so that in harmony with the rising Rooseveltian economy we all seemed to be riding a special rainbow to the Good Life, Rexito and Burt and Garland and Larry, blessed children of this most blessed land.

All of the humiliations of bygone years had been erased, all the Harry Viners dispatched to the dustbins of history. Horatio Alger was real, all right. There was no justification for skepticism, because the evidence that we were annointed was simply overwhelming.

But even the elect must labor at their calling, especially during a depression. In the Knot Hole Gang, you could pick up empty Coke bottles off the concrete tiers and take them to a drugstore not too far away from the stadium. You got two cents a bottle. Burt and Rexito and I used to pick up Coke bottles at the end of games, as many as we could carry, eight or nine if you worked at it carefully, and with this we mobilized enough capital for a postgame malted milk—if you didn't drop too many on the concrete tiers. It is mid-October of 1939—the sophomore year—and the Texas Longhorns, though now obviously on the road back, are losing to Arkansas 13–7 with thirty seconds to play. I am distracting myself from total despair by scavenging relentlessly. I now have a record number of fourteen Coke bottles in my arms.

Suddenly, there goes Crain, Jack Crain, Cowboy Crain, the Nocona Nugget, breaking to the outside, his 170-pound frame flashing past the secondary, skipping around those last two men, into the open—seventy yards for a touchdown. After frenzied spectators are cleared from the field, Crain "calmly" (that's what the paper said) kicks the extra point that brings Texas a 14–13 victory. On the way up, Horatio!

What I remember is that when Cowboy Jack started upfield I had all fourteen Coke bottles in my arms. I may have had them when he blurred past the last two Arkansas players. Then Burt Newlove is leaping on the seats in front of us and letting go a wild cry of utter triumph, and Rexito and I are jumping up and down in each other's arms. When they tried to clear the field for the extra point, I discovered we were standing in about two inches of broken Coke bottles. It didn't matter. Glory and wonder in your eleventh year on the planet has no room for twenty-eight-cent setbacks. Our tragedies were subsumed in our blessedness.

Our childhood began to come to an end on a November day in 1941 when the impossible happened, when the Wonder Team, the *Life* magazine cover team, was upset 14–7 by TCU, a day when Malcolm Kutner dropped a Pete Layden pass on the goal line, when Jack Crain slipped while breaking into the open. A jagged tear in the lining, one November afternoon in another century.

In the fading moments of that game, I remember learning something about religion, a subject in which I had not had much prior training. You prayed when things were out of your hands. "Catch it, Malcolm," I prayed; then, that he would catch the next one. I prayed for Pete Layden to throw the next one. "Oh Lord, if You'll just let Texas win, I promise I'll. . . ." The passionate bargains of the powerless. Horatio?

The end, the very end, was full of meaning that we did not recognize. While the Wonder Team was thrashing almost everybody, and losing to TCU and tying Baylor, the little old Aggies were edging by people, so that when we met them on Thanksgiving Day, the unbeaten Aggies were already champions. They were the number two team in the nation, right behind Minnesota. It left us all a bit dazed. So the 23–0 Texas win over A&M was not the high moment of celebration it might have been. We were still only second in our own conference. It seemed impossible. It was like a soaring glider had come to rest in the middle of the sky. Things are just not supposed to end that way.

THERE WAS A FATEFUL POSTSCRIPT. TEXAS, BREAKING precedent, had scheduled a game after Thanksgiving. It came against Oregon, a team that had just missed going to the Rose Bowl. At the end, in that final performance, the Longhorns were never more magnificent. It was as if the shattered dreams were somehow, for an instant, reassembled through one last blinding display of pure artistry and excellence. The Wonder Team was breathtaking. The final score was 71–7. From the Knot Hole Gang, it looked—and was—awesome. Yet it was not enough. The season was over, and the ultimate glory of the National Championship had slipped away somehow. The play had closed, to disappointed theatre goers. In Sonora and Rawls and in Jack Crain's hometown of Nocona, where West Texas boys had made the cover of *Life* magazine, the people sat around and speculated about what *should* have been. And in Austin, Rexito and Burt and Garland and I would start sentences, "If only Kutner had. . . ."

On the night the season ended, when the might-have-beens began, my father consoled us that "in the larger perspective" our difficulty was manageable. We learned, rather soon, that he was right.

The date of the Oregon game was December 6, 1941. We were thirteen.

NINE

We Were Profes- sionals

LOU HOLLOWAY AND ALFERDTEEN HARRISON

FOR MANY CHILDREN,
music is one of the
extracurricular activities that
come with going to school.
For some black students across
the South, music also provided
a way to raise money for their
own schools when the
segregated school system failed
to provide an education. In
one famous example, the Fisk
University Jubilee Singers,
founded in 1871, raised
$100,000 in their first three
years of existence. Jubilee Hall,
built in 1876 with the
proceeds from early tours, was
the first permanent building in
the South for the education of
blacks. In Mississippi, just
outside of Jackson, the Piney
Woods School survived
because of the money brought
in by a whole range of student
activities, but most notably
from its female jazz bands, the
Sweethearts of Rhythm and
the Rays of Rhythm.

The Piney Woods School
was founded in 1909 to
provide a high school
education and training for jobs
to black students from the
rural counties surrounding
Jackson. Under the leadership
of Laurence C. Jones, the
school's founder, Piney Woods
emerged as a positive
community force in the lives
of the black and white people
of Mississippi.

The need for private schools
for black children was clear.
When Mississippi segregated its
schools by state law in 1890,
little pretense was made of
providing equal education to
the races. In 1910, the year

65

after Piney Woods was founded, only 64 percent of black children attended school, compared to 84 percent of white children. The illiteracy rate for blacks was seven times that for whites, reflecting the fact that about five times as much was spent to educate each white child as was spent to educate each black child. By 1929, thirty-nine counties still had no high school for black children, and in 1939 the spending ratio had worsened to ten to one. One Mississippi county in 1939 spent $42.97 on the education of each white child, and $1 on the education of each black child. *

The female jazz groups were organized by Dr. Jones after a male dance band had experienced great success. The Sweethearts of Rhythm and subsequently the Rays of Rhythm became famous from Alabama to Texas, bringing high-quality big-band jazz to Southern night clubs and earning as much as $400 a night for the Piney Woods School.

I REMEMBER, IN THE FALL WE WOULD PICK COTTON. MY father would say, "If you pick this cotton and you make good, you get this cotton out"—he'd always promise to take us up to Piney Woods School for their commencement in the spring.

And I would always come back, and the rest of the week or months I would just daydream about getting back up there. And I remember that summer when postcards were one cent. I got a postcard and sent it to the president, Dr. Jones, and said that I wanted to come to Piney Woods School and said that I wanted to play in the band.

My first job was in the dining hall, washing dishes, that's usually what you do. Then you begin to get your work assignments. I wanted to play an instrument. I guess maybe after Christmas I start playing instruments, you know, taking up music. I started saxophone, I learned my scales.

I remember we'd come upstairs from eating dinner and all girls, especially new girls were practicing after dinner. Cause they would eat early and we would hear them practicing upstairs while we were eating downstairs. Just swinging away, you know. When you come up you would stand at the screens there and watch and look.

So, I started taking music. When I started, instead of practicing the exercises, I started hearing songs and I'd just pick them out on my horn, then begin to play. I will never

*See: Charles H. Wilson, *Education for Negroes in Mississippi Since 1910* (Boston: Meador, 1947) and 1910 Census of Population.

forget the number, this thing called, "At Last My Love."
(Sings it.) And I was just playing that on the alto sax and
the guy came in, cause it was time for my music lessons.
And he started with the music lessons and about two
weeks later he wrote something very simple for me that
was a jazz kind of thing.

There were three groups, Sweethearts of Rhythm, Rays
of Rhythm, and the Flashers. When I got there the
Sweethearts had already gone off professionally. They ran
away from the school. Then the Rays of Rhythm had to
pick up their itinerary, you see, take on the dates that they
had for the school, when they left. Then under the Rays of
Rhythm there was an understudy group called the Flashers
of Rhythm.

[Before the Sweethearts ran away] the Kays practiced at
home every evening, because if a girl who plays saxophone
gets sick on the road, you take a girl out of the Rays to
replace that girl. The understudy group practiced the same
book, that's what they called it, all the same music. So all
those dates that had been booked when the Sweethearts
cut away from the school couldn't be filled, so the Rays of
Rhythm were sent out to fill those dates. And they became
the traveling group for Piney Woods.

IN MAY, EVERY GROUP—THE BALL TEAMS, THE QUARTETS,
the bands—was equipped out and provisioned out in those
traveling buses going their different directions. You didn't
see them until September, because they had to raise money
to keep the school going.

About 1942 or 1943, there was a show, just one of
those black shows, a road show called the Silas Green
Road Show. Somehow Dr. Jones met the manager of Silas
Green and made a deal for the Rays of Rhythm to travel
with that show. Dr. Jones split up that band, took some of
them and sent them with the Silas Green Show. They were
still getting the same money that they got just like those
quartets, so much a day, a dollar a day, to buy hair oil and
toothpaste and stuff like that. I think he paid them a little
more, but the bulk of the money still came to the school. I
think they must have stayed out there about a year.

We were professional. We were playing dances. People were booking that band. Thanksgiving Eve and Thanksgiving Day, Christmas Eve and Christmas Day, the Easter Weekend, we didn't have to worry. One man booked us [every year], we always knew that. But we would go there and play for him and then we keep on up through Louisiana, up through Arkansas, back down through the Delta of Mississippi. Playing one night, we never did have to travel more than fifty miles.

Dances usually started at nine o'clock at night. We played four-hour dances. Now, musicians come to Jackson, they play a show, maybe an hour or twenty minutes and that's it. You paying that big money. We played four hours with a thirty-minute intermission. Which is the same thing that Duke Ellington, Count Basie and all the other bands were doing. One o'clock we were off.

When we would go in to play, we could set up our own bandstand. Now, the business manager and the driver would bring all the stuff and they would set up the heavy stuff. We didn't have to lift the big things. But as far as adjusting that microphone, doing all that, we did it.

At intermission we came back to the bus. We did not socialize with the public because we were under age. See, when I was in the band the average age was seventeen. When I started I was fourteen. People could come up and ask for a number or request or something, but we could not just have a conversation. We were there to entertain the people and not to socialize. We were to play for the dance and that's it.

You'd go back at the bus at intermission and we had a refrigerator box. We'd eat out only at restaurants during the day. But after the dance we didn't hardly ever eat at restaurants, unless we playing in Jackson. [The manager] sat all of us together and was going to see that, you know, nobody uses profanity because we were kids. We would have milk and a small sandwich or some cookies, you know, or some fruit. We didn't eat many sweets because we had to blow a horn and that would take your wind away you know.

After we finished we'd go back after thirty minutes and play another hour and then you're through. You come back when you get your instrument together. We'd get on the bus, take off our uniforms, get ready for bed.

We had jazzie uniforms. Now we were wearing pants on the stage when other people were not wearing pants. We had black satin pants with a green satin sash with gold fringe on the end of it, and gold satin blouses with big puff sleeves. In the summer, we had some navy blue pants, with cotton blouses with navy blue stripes or pokie dots in it to blend with it and blue or red sash. Never dresses, always pants.

I remember going into the Rose Room in Vicksburg. It was a beautiful room, a fabulous place, something like Stevens' Rose Room in Jackson but it's bigger. You come in that door at the stairs and look on that stage, oh! Those 16 girls and all that pretty satin, and always all gold instruments, no silver instruments unless there was an emergency. People would come in, "Ah, those girls can play." 'Cause it was novelty for girls to play that kind of music. And so then we would come up with a theme song and start (popping fingers) and just rock the place, you know.

We slept on the bus, one bunk was here, another one right up by the window, another one up there. Three tiers, enough for two girls on each tier. Right down here in the lobby of the thing was a pullout where the manager and the chaperone slept. Then there was another bed for the girls. Instruments, drums, and things were in the back of the bus. Had our own toilet on board that had to be emptied. The driver would empty that at night as we moved. Then you had these wash basins, that you used to wash up with. And there was a place for towels and things like that to be stacked. And each girl had a drawer to keep all your stuff in. You had to make up your beds before you left, clean up the trailer. People used to come over to look, just take a tour.

DR. JONES LOVED THAT JAZZ BAND. A LOT OF THE FOLKS wanted to get rid of the band, they didn't agree with it. He would always defend us. If you got in that band, you got by with murder. I guess he understood that, number one, we were kids, number two, every time you go off you are seeing something exciting. You come back and you recap it. "Hey, remember that night, we were in such-a-such place and that person did this, or something." So, you start talking, because we could talk out loud on the bus like that. But when we got in the dormitory, we got just a little loud and we'd start laughing.

I guess one reason we loved Dr. Jones, his chastising was different from any of the rest of them. He didn't shout and scold. He just sat down and he reasoned and explained, "Now, you're out here, you can't do this, the reason why you don't do this. . . ." So, we didn't mind it when he came.

People used to complain, "You just buy those band girls

all that." But we brought money into that school. If we played a dance one night, we got $225. By the time you took care of gas, bought our food, and paid us our allowance, you've got $150 there, every day. That's daily. I'm sure—unless we had to buy a tire or something like that or the bus broke down—every day we must have cleared $100 to $150. We're out there three weeks. So each month we must have brought $2,000, $3,000 into that school. So that could pay salaries, right? That could do a lot of things.

One thing that Dr. Jones said to me and a couple of other girls was—we were talking about the attitudes of the people—and he said, "Well, you know, sometimes

Father (Earl) Hines and the Swinging Rays of Rhythm

people can't see so far, but you go on and do this because you're doing this to get through school, so you can go out there and do something. The other girls are doing something else. So just remember you're doing the same thing to go out there and be a good secretary if you're taking typing or whatever you're going to do."

And I still say to people when I get a job now, I know how to do things. I can go back and play some blues right now, if necessary, if I had to eat.

TEN

Two Stories

DANNY GAFFORD

Home Run Lie

BACK WHEN I WAS
eleven or twelve years old, I
wasn't really interested in sports
at all, and when I did play I
was so nervous because I was
scared I'd make a mistake, that
I wasn't any good, so I didn't
play sports that much.

Well it started one day. You
see my Dad was a member of
the VFW Club, and the
members decided to start a
little league baseball team, and
since my Dad thought I would
enjoy it, I got signed up
without me knowing anything
about it! By all the practice all
us kids had, the coach knew I
wasn't any good but every
game we would play I was
always sitting on the bench. But
I had a plan. I would tell my
Dad not to come to the games,
because him being there would
make me nervous, and I
couldn't play good, but really I
didn't want him to know how
rotten I was! But the last game
of the season the coach put me
in, I played right field, and I'm
glad no balls came to me, but I
still had to bat. The pitcher
threw the first ball, I swung
with all my might, and I missed
the ball, second pitch I swung
and hit the ball, but it went foul
for strike 2, third pitch I swung
and missed the ball for strike 3
(I'm out)! When I went home
later my Dad asked me did I
play tonight, and I wanted to
make him proud of me so I
told him I hit a home run, and
my Dad patted me on the back,
and said Good Boy! The next

73

morning my sister told me that Daddy sat by the radio last night and listened to the whole game. But my Dad never said anything about that lie I told him about "Hitting the Home Run!"

Love Hurts Forever

WHEN I WAS 17 TEEN, AND LIVEING IN DICKSON, TENNESSEE (a very small town—pop. 20,000), the thing was to drive around in your car haveing fun like, chaseing girls, showing how bad your car was, chaseing more girls, drinking beer, wine, & takeing or smokeing dope, and chaseing more girls. This only happened on Friday nights, but Saturday nights was a little more special—on Saturday night you done everything you done on Friday night, but if you hadn't caught a date by 11:00 at night, you could always go to the skating rink and get a date for the rest of the night. Well this Saturday night Bob, Steve, Billy, Phil, Mike, Elton & myself all had to go to the skating rink! You see on Saturday night at the rink, they skate until 12:00 midnight, then the live band sits up on the floor, and the skating rink turns into a "wild" Dance Party. By 12:00 Steve, Phil, Mike had dates and left. By 12:30 Elton, Billy had to go home, so that left Bob & myself to get dates; now Bob is kind of weird—meaning just dum; for myself I take it a little slower, I like to look around before I approach anyone, but this time I saw her before seeing anyone else; she was leaning against the wall with some other girls. I turned to Bob, and told him he had to fined another way home, then I turned around to fined her, but she was dancing with some dude, but I wasn't giving up, I started walking toward them, and stop right beside them and told the guy thanks for watching my girl and he stepped back from her, and I stepped in and started dancing with her & he walk away. Now she stopped dancing and said, "Why did you do that?" and I said keep dancing, and she did, & I told her my name & she told me hers. Well, we danced, & talked intill the dance was over, then I took her home in my car; when we got to her Mother's house we made plans for another date Sunday night, and then we kissed and said good night, and she got out & went in, then I pulled out of the driveway and went home.

After three or four months of dating we were very close, we had made beautiful love many times, been to the drive-in, (It was called the Hot-Pit when I was growing up), been to Nashville & Memphis, Tenn. many times—we was together more than married people was, intill I got a job to support myself, & my dates! I worked for my brother-in-law which own a construction comp., and we worked at Clarksville, Tenn. on a college. On payday (Friday), I asked my brother-in-law for my pay check at lunch time, where I could cash it where I could buy some lunch, but he was drunk, and started saying bad things about my girl to the other workers, so I took my check from him, got into my car, and went to cash the check which was $246.37 and drove straight to my girl's house, and told her that I moved out of my Dad's house (you see my sister and brother-in-law lived with my Dad). So my girl asked me to stay with her, & I did.

My Dad called every day, but I always told my girl to tell him I wasn't there, intill one day I talked to him. He wanted me to come home, but I told him not intill we talked first. He said he would pick me up & I said, No, we would meet somewhere, and he said OK; we met at the coffee shop; after a long talk I decided to go get my stuff & move, but when I got home I called my girl and told her I was going to stay home, but would see her that night. When I saw my girl that night we went dancing at the skating rink, when we were dancing to a slow dance I told her I loved her, & wish we could get married, but I couldn't afford to get married because I didn't have a job anymore; I took her to her house about 3:00 in the morning, and we dated three or four more times intill she had a car wreck, and I went to the hospital to see her, and she told me she losted the baby, and told me to leave before her mother got there, because she didn't like me anymore, so I left, and didn't see her again intill I meet her husband. But now she divorced, and I still wish I could dance with her one more time at the skating rink and tell her I still "Love her very much!"

ELEVEN

Something in the Pastrami

RUBY LERNER

LACKING ROOTS, ALIENS must learn to live by their wits. Fortunately, Southern women are raised with a truly horrifying set of skills—the ability to get exactly what they want through the most devious means available. It could be something in the water supply. And fortunately, Jews are raised with an unquestionable instinct for survival. It must be something in the pastrami.

1955: A PICKY EATER, I tried desperately with the few words at my seven-year-old command to describe ham to my mother. We never had it at home, in Lenoir, North Carolina, but we got it at school, and I lived for it—this wondrous, exotic, salty meat.

1959: When I was eleven, my best friend Marsha told me I'd be real popular if I'd learn how to dance and roll my hair. I did both.

1960: Daddy forbade me to take the New Testament Bible class that was part of the junior high curriculum, so I stayed in homeroom and mastered yet-to-be-uttered words like eleemosynary and pterodactyl for local spelling bees. I began to savor the prospect of being a heathen. With not a prayer for salvation.

1968: I chose to major in comparative religion.

1958–1964: We drove all the way to Charlotte (about

ninety miles away) every Sunday for Sunday school. My father was determined to inject his offspring with some Jewishness in that Southern Baptismal wilderness. I suspect I was a stranger creature to those city Jews than I was at home. I was certainly more interested in boys than in Hebrew, but since I didn't live in Charlotte, I was mostly excluded from the social whirl. An alien, albeit in Weejuns, Villagers, and circle pins.

1964–1966: Now, there was a Jewish center in Hickory (only about twenty miles away), and we had to go to Sabbath services. Every Friday night. Of course, Friday night is *the* high school football night, which is *the* social event of the week, and I missed almost every game. I began to get hateful.

1980: I still don't understand the first thing about football.

1966: Although voted "Most Likely to Succeed"—by one vote (my best friend and also contender for the title voted for me)—I did not make it to the Homecoming Court.

High-School Sophomores and Seniors in Central Texas

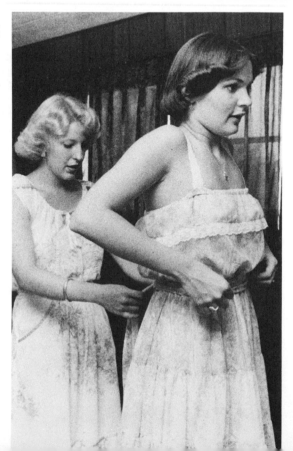

Ruby Lerner and Family

1980: I have never recovered from this.

1966: I did, however, make it to the North Carolina Jewish Debutante Ball.

1980: I have no memory of that event.

1966–1970: I always believed that ''life'' would not begin until I made my escape from the xenophobic South. So I headed north to Baltimore. But my Long Island Jewish Princess roommate thought she would *die* every time I said something intelligent with a Southern accent. She was shocked to find that I had a working knowledge of water faucets and also knew enough about electricity to recognize a wall outlet.

1970: Homesick, I longed for North Carolina. Homesick, I came home.

1974: Dear Ruby, I can't make it to Chapel Hill this weekend. I'm not feeling well. Maggie isn't doing well either. One side is completely paralyzed, and she can't talk plain. Well, that's the way we're all going to go. Your father and I don't have many years to go either. Love, Mom.

LENOIR. ALICE IS HOME. HER FATHER RECENTLY DEAD. HER mother with career. We look at photos of her father fishing, her father at the Moose Lodge, her mother graduating. She shows me a stack of faded ribboned letters that certify her Mayflower past, her rootedness in the land, proof of her American nobility.

My ghosts are here. Separate from the ghosts of my father, which dwell in the Carpathians, and the ghosts of my mother, which lurk in Berlin. My parents cannot understand this—that *my* ghosts are here. Even when they elude me, I am certain they own the key to my being whole.

I walk down the streets where I contemplated suicide at the age of twelve.

After my day with Alice, I search for signs of my own nobility. Scion of wanderers, I am just as documented. I grasp at old photographs, but they mean nothing. A grandmother on her way to butchery by the Nazis? A cousin snapped at a bar mitzvah? The contemporary Polaroids among them are jarring. I cannot identify those faces either.

Lacking information, I am at sea. Dispossessed of this tribal continuum.

I become frantic. Posterity. Who will say of me, of my faded photograph, wasn't she beautiful? As a friend confessed to me that she always had a crush on my father, will someone confess these same thoughts to my son ten years after the fact, then years after the beauty?

Who knows what even to wish for? Beauty? Sons? Confession?

THERE'S A KIND OF FREEDOM IN BEING AN ALIEN. SINCE nobody expects you to behave appropriately in the first place, all outrages, if not quite tolerated, are at least comprehensible.

I have taken to identifying myself as a Southern Jewess.

I expect this to explain any discernible tragic flaws.

TWELVE
Delicate Con-
versations

MAB SEGREST

IT IS THE SECOND GRADE.
I am at a senior high football
game, at the ball field a few
blocks from my house in a
small Alabama town. I am not
watching the game but playing
with my brother and his
friends, since I always play
with them. I can go anywhere
if I do; otherwise, I have to
stay at home. We are throwing
rocks at some of the girls in
my brother John's room at
school. The girls are on the
bleachers; we are underneath,
looking up at their underpants.
I have a crush on one of them
—Rebecca, dark eyes and hair,
smart and full-bosomed
already, in the fourth grade. I
like her a lot, so I am throwing
rocks at her. Then she says,
pointing at me, "Look at Mab,
she's on the wrong side." I
stop, terrified, and go and sit
next to my parents in silence
for the rest of the ball game. I
am quiet during the cakewalk
afterwards, and the walk
home. I do not know which
side won. That night in the
bathtub I begin to cry. My
mother says, "Honey, what's
the matter?" Watching the
dirty water flecked with
soapsuds, I tell her what
Rebecca said. My mother is
silent, and I say, sobbing, "I
want to be a girl." And my
mother says, "You can be,"
and I wish she had said,
"You are."

MY BEST SUNDAY SCHOOL
friend Amy Watters, on a
humid summer afternoon
between the second and third

grade, began my initiation into the terrifying knowledge of sex. Amy's mother, usually at least half-crazy, had broken the news to Amy that morning, and Amy had raced over immediately after lunch, figuring that this was something I did not know. She was right.

"So you see," she triumphantly announced (she was just going into first grade and delighted to know something I didn't), "the man sticks his peter in the woman's pee-pee and they have a baby."

I had been dodging cracks in the pavement (step on a crack and you have to get married). I stopped still. I was immediately offended that Amy had said "peter" and "pee-pee," which I knew were dirty words, instead of "wee-wee" for both, like John and I did. Then it struck me what else Amy had said.

"That isn't true," I replied with equal confidence. I knew that a man's wee-wee couldn't fit into a woman's wee-wee and felt sorry that Amy had such a crazy mother.

"But it is, the man sticks his—"

I stopped her from repeating it again. *"My* momma and daddy don't do that," I said, trying to convince myself that maybe this was just something that affected children whose mothers worked in the sewing factory.

Amy was relentless. "Yes they do, too, my momma says *everybody's* mommas and daddies do."

I had a sudden feeling it was true. My universe teetered near the heart of a vast darkness as I saw millions of daddies, including my own, wee-weeing in millions of mommas instead of in their toilets. I had watched my brother urinate many times, his hand guiding the soft stream of water into the porcelain bowl, although I had to climb onto the lowered seat and hold on tight to keep from falling in. And sometimes at night, especially in the winter, when I was comfortable in my bed, I would dream I was already on the toilet seat, dreaming carefully the entire stumble around the corner of the bed, through the opened door, around the clothes hamper to the chilly toilet—then I would wet the bed, waking up damp and ashamed but also relieved at having avoided the darkened bathroom and the frozen floor. How any of this related to babies, I could not understand. I knew very well, like I knew to say "yes, ma'am'' and ''no, sir'' and ''Please and thank you,'' that wee-wee and do-do and toilets went together and that it was embarrassing and shameful and probably a sin to do it anywhere else, and this had something to do with why we had to wear pants over our seats even in summer heat and why mother had gotten so upset when Kevin White persuaded my little sister to pull down her underpants on the sidewalk, even when she didn't mind. I was humiliated that my parents might do this when they had told me not to and confused that they would hide it from me, suddenly terrified at living in a world where this happened at least as often as there were children, and even more afraid of what other ugly truths my parents might have concealed. Finally, I was not a little upset at God for having arranged things in such a nasty fashion, and later in Sunday school when I heard about the Virgin birth, I saw that God had found the process distasteful also and had devised for Himself, anyway, a method of getting around it.

So I went around in a panic for all of June, not speaking to my parents except to be polite, and hardly talking to John, either, since I wanted to spare him this knowledge, until I convinced myself that what Amy had revealed must not be that important or true, or my mother would have told me about it. With great relief I forgot about sex for as long as I could. I reverted to my old belief that babies were born because God, and sometimes Jesus, sprinkled stardust out of heaven, like Tinkerbell in *Peter Pan,* and when this dust floated down onto possible mothers, they had babies. I had heard my friends Lana Williams and Marcy Franklin talk in whispers about unwed mothers, and I figured that for them God had missed or been poorly informed about who was married and when—which I could understand since heaven was so far up in the sky that God couldn't be expected to see or hear about everything, or to have perfect aim.

The stardust theory kept me safe for another few years. The next step in my education came from the unlikely combination of my grandmother Mab and the novel *Adam Bede.* By that time, my grandmother was seventy, and senility had begun to overcome Victorian reticence and hone her lifelong frankness into a near brutal naivete that could reveal to grandchildren in minutes what parents had taken years to conceal. Her vision was failing, and a friend had arranged for her to get what they called "talking books," records from the Institute for the Blind that arrived periodically in black metal boxes. I liked to climb upstairs in the slow heavy hours after summer lunch to my grandmother's room, its four windows open, mimosa branches tapping panes, and mahogany furniture weighting the afternoon. Listening to Victorian novels, I could sometimes glimpse behind my toothless grandmother gnome, her chin always lightly gumming the air, a younger woman-creature, clean limbed and walking with her children in the Chatauqua grass. When I missed an afternoon's reading, she would offer a brief synopsis, and it was in one of these pauses as the Victrola needle scratched towards its place that my grandmother explained how Arthur had made Hetty "so that she would have a baby," me standing in the doorway between the bathroom and the bedroom, finding myself shocked again that men had anything to do with babies. Wondering what it could be.

About this time, having read an article in *Ladies Day* at the beauty parlor, my mother failed her only weak attempt at sex education. The *Ladies Day* writer explained that enlightened parents simply gave their children enlightened books, thus relieving them of the awkward necessity of explaining sexual intercourse, and it recommended two volumes, *For Girls Only* and *For Boys Only.* I read my volume dutifully in an afternoon, lying slantwise on my bed, feet propped against the wall. I learned all about ovaries and eggs and monthly periods and absolutely everything that the sperm does after it finds itself inexplicably in the vagina: the desperate swim up the fallopian tubes, one terrified little tadpole consummating its pilgrimage to the huge egg-shrine, looming up ahead, luminous and absorbing, to be engulfed. Then came the nine months, called "gestation," in stages like chicken eggs opened every three days at school, then the clench and release of muscled darkness, now the baby swimming toward the light. It all made perfect sense to me as I put the book down and went to my parents' bedroom, where my mother was making the bed.

"Through already?" my mother asked.

"Yes, ma'am," proud at my speed.

"Any questions?" my mother the teacher now, feeling safe.

I brightened, glad that I knew the obvious question to ask. "Well, I understand what they said about the egg and all, but there's one thing I don't understand. . . ."

"Yes," my mother more tentative now, realizing she had not read the book.

"I see how the . . . sperm . . . gets to the . . . egg—but how does the sperm get in the lady in the first place?"

My mother paused, mid-pillow. She breathed in and out and turned to reach for a clean pillowcase and answered over her shoulder in defeat, "Ask your father." Since I was not in the habit of conducting delicate conversations with my father over sperms and eggs, I knew this explanation would just have to wait.

At this point, my mother should have given up on being an enlightened parent, but she persevered, following the next *Ladies Day* recommendation, and had my brother and me swap books. So next I set to reading all about testicles and penises and scrotums and urethras and glands, and about how boys shouldn't worry if their testicles were huge or their penises infinitesimal. And for two years after, I could never look a boy my age in the face; my eyes were riveted to their crotches, and the sweat and the urine smell of male locker rooms filled my fantasies with penises that hung past knees.

LIGHT FINALLY BROKE FOR ME ON THE MECHANICS OF SEX, most appropriately, at a Girl Scout meeting. My troop was on its way back from Montgomery, where we had gone to be on Cartoon Carl's TV show. I was in the back seat with my best friends at that time, Marcy and Lana. Both (at twelve years old) with boyfriends in senior high school, they conducted secret conversations that I was not privy to. I felt that they knew more of the way of the world than I did, and I found them wise and dangerous and vulnerable in a way that I loved. They were drawn to me for my ignorant innocence. This afternoon we were rocking along in the back seat of Rudy Goggins's station wagon, Girl Scout greens bedraggled, badge sashes awry, telling jokes, and giggling past a blur of cotton fields and Nehi signs.

Lana's turn. "Here's one my brother told me." We all turned quiet and expectant.

"See, this man and woman were on their honeymoon, and they took off their clothes, and the man said, 'What's that,' and the woman said, 'Mountains,' and the woman said, 'What's that?' and the man said, 'The Lone Ranger,' and the man said, 'What's that?' and the woman said, 'Lonesome Valley,' and that night the clouds rolled over the mountains and the Lone Ranger rode into Lonesome Valley."

After a silent moment we all chortled loudly, and I sat there and looked out the window and finally knew.

Another scene: Marcy and Lana and I sit on a swing under the pecan tree in Marcy's backyard. We are tentatively swinging, feet fretting the ground. Lana is rubbing her palms, crisscrossed with a hundred tiny lines, creases ancient and sorrowful and incongruous on a twelve-year-old. She is saying that her mother has told her that so many wrinkles on her hands means she will die young.

Marcy turns suddenly to me. "Has your mother told you about sex?"

I think about *For Girls Only* but know that isn't what she means and lie, "Yes."

Marcy: "Can I tell you a secret?"

Me: "Yes."

Marcy: "Promise you won't tell?"

I nod.

"My mother told my brothers and me about . . . it . . . and they wanted to see what it was like and . . . they did it to me." She pauses, leaning forward in the tire swing. "But it's OK, since I'm their sister . . . isn't it?"

I understand only the urgency in Marcy's question, feel in it a request for absolution of deeds beyond my capacity to imagine. Just then her brother Bill walks out the back door, stopping still on the top porch step. The three of us look over, and he catches Marcy's eye and holds it for a full ominous moment before his head flicks and he bounds out of the yard. Marcy is looking at the ground now, and I lean forward and say, "Yeah, sure Marcy, yeah, sure it's OK."

Beauty Pageant in West-Central Texas

THIRTEEN

Nigger-Knocking

ROBERT HOUSTON

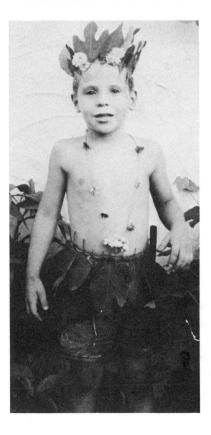

IT IS AN ODD TRUTH THAT most anything that *is* in one's childhood is accepted as the natural order of things. Causation is assigned only in retrospect. And so I suppose the varieties of nigger-knocking should be remembered as they were, and as I accepted them, and I must be left to attempt to absolve my guilt in private insurrections.

Nigger-knocking, like fighting to bring blood, was a phenomenon of my freshman year in high school and in a sense was bound up in a whole social milieu. In that larger world after grammar school, my social inadequacies were mercilessly revealed: success and status, with a kind of Alabama populism, were denied to both ends of all spectrums. The rich and the poor, the liberal and the Klansman, the brute and the intellectual—all were suspect in a pseudogenteel world whose mists of propriety made all distinct outlines crepuscular. So with a terrible new fear of distinction, I resolved to become invisible. One could not be a Baptist, I discovered right away, and be a success. Baptism was too conspicuous, too raw and reminiscent of the all-too-recent immigration of one's grandparents into Birmingham from the mining camps. I was willing enough to change, and there was at least no problem of alternatives. Catholicism was unheard of; Episcopalianism was an affectation; Presbyterianism was

89

alien and Tennesseeish. Methodism, the middle ground, was the only choice. And so I converted, covering as best I could my other inadequacies—to wit, my father wasn't a professional man; my mother smoked Camels, worked, and didn't plant flowers; and I had never been nigger-knocking.

Since nigger-knocking, the initiation ceremony, was a regular Sunday night ritual after Methodist Youth Fellowship, it was a problem whose solution was implied in conversion, and the others I could lie about. Having been nigger-knocking, I would have proven myself and would become a "good old boy," my most coveted appellation.

The connection between Methodism and nigger-knocking was, it seems now, a reasonable enough one. Birmingham Sunday nights are nightmares of boredom. Baptist fervor could spend at least enough energy to make them tolerable, but Methodist restraint was only a catalyst. At nine o'clock on a summer Sunday evening, with a father's car on one hand (Methodist fathers had cars), seduced by the moist Southern night and keyed up from a weekend of dates with chaste Methodist girls, some sort of action was a gut necessity. And since everything in town was blue-lawed, and the quarters were near, and nigger-knocking had about it the air of cause as well as excitement, I suppose it was the logical choice of outlets. Not that there was any real danger involved, of course, since one was always near enough to a white section for easy refuge, and few blacks had cars anyway. But there was the joy of the hunt about it.

Methodism, nigger-knocking, and I enjoyed a relatively brief partnership, but one that lasted long enough to allow me to learn most of the refinements of the art (although I never did learn the religion, being driven away for drinking beer in public before I even had the chance to memorize all of the Apostles' Creed). And, as best I can recall, the equipment and techniques of a typical Sunday night foray were roughly as follows.

We would gather behind the church, usually in a group of four or five—four being the ideal number, since everyone could then have his own window, and no one would feel slighted. The most basic and available ammunition, rocks, could be laid in on the spot from around the unpaved parking lot, so that before we left, each of us had his own reserve stores. But the more sophisticated weapons were what we were really after, and these demanded more careful gathering.

There were, for instance, clay pots, to be swiped from the florist's yard on Seventy-seventh Street, as a start. These had the ballistic advantage of throwing well and shattering loudly, so that even if there were no direct hits, the target was sufficiently terrified for us to feel the sally successful. (The image of three Negro girls, neat in white starched Sunday dresses, leaping and screaming and covering their faces as the pots shattered all around them, distills itself from one particularly successful run. And as we sped away, screeching around the next corner, laughing, we thought it all the better when, vanishing behind us, the oldest girl screamed, "You motherfuckers, you motherfuckers, you rotten motherfuckers. . . ." It was proof of white superiority.)

Next to rocks and pots, water balloons were probably our most popular munitions. They were relatively harmless —or at least not potentially fatal—and they admitted to interesting variations. They could, when thrown from a car at forty miles an hour, stun with a direct hit and produce a grand fallout area even with a miss. For Panama suits, there were balloons with ink in the water, and for girls, the ultimate: piss in the water. (Again, an image: an old man with a cane, alone, caught from behind as he walked past a weedy vacant lot. With rebel yells and unusual accuracy —three out of four balloons, direct hits—and the old man toppling slowly and stiffly, like a radio tower in a storm, into the weeds. And with no look of surprise at all on his face, before the distance and the dust behind us on the dirt road wiped him out of sight.)

But probably the subtlest, most accurate, and most imaginative weapon of all was the simplest and easiest to use. Automobile radio aerials were no trouble to steal and could be carried in a ready position almost invisibly and discarded instantly if need be. The only trouble with aerials, though, was finding proper quarry. The object, of course, was to find game walking close enough to the street, since the aerial's reach was, unfortunately, a bit limited. And one had to be accurate enough to avoid necks and faces, since that would be *too* cruel at forty or fifty miles an hour. At any rate, when a target was found, all that was needed was a wrist movement, and the aerial would be extended perpendicular to the car, back high, and would hit with a resounding splat that could draw blood from a bare back and raise, we were sure, delicious whelps on a covered one.

There were, of course, other refinements, though becoming *too* visionary in seeking new methods could in fact often do more harm than good—as I remember from the night we decided to add psychological nuance to our hunt. Police sirens, we all knew, tended to produce immediate and varied responses from Negroes. So that evening, we cruised through the downtown quarters strewing the usual balloons, pots, and rocks, but spicing things considerably by doing our best siren imitations all the while. This was a reasonably interesting thing to do, granted, but stupid in that it was encroaching on posted territory, and policemen are jealous guardians.

They had kept us in sight for some time apparently, and, as we pulled into an alley behind the Thomas Jefferson Hotel to take a piss, they caught us, literally, with our pants down (or at least unzipped). Their white car hissing around the building so suddenly—policemen love dramatic entrances—left us with no choice but to freeze.

"Y'all boys stay where you are," said the driver from behind the headlights, with a voice as deep and authoritative as the Methodist God's must be.

The lights went out, two doors slammed, and the policemen sauntered over to us. With terrifying flashlights, they silently looked us over.

"Zip your pants up," ordered the driver.

We complied, fumbling.

"Pretty good at sirening, ain't you, boys?" said the other.

"Having a pretty good time, wudn't you?" rumbled the driver.

"Yessir, I guess," I said finally, trying to look sheepish.

" 'Bout to get in trouble with it, too, boy. I'll tell you that for one thing. We been keeping up with you," he answered.

"Yessir."

"Yessir, hell! Y'all ever one disgust me, you know that? Plain disgust me."

"Why is that sir?"

"Why? Goddamn, boy! How would you like yo' mamma to walk by and see somebody pissing on the street like that, huh? Like a animal!"

"Plain disgusting," his partner said.

Later, I understand, there were assassinations.

FOURTEEN

How Can You Tell?

HONOREE F. JEFFERS, AGE 12, 1980

IT WAS A BOY. THE midwife held it up so Martha could see him. Although Martha was very dark, the baby boy was the color of milk.

Martha had hoped that the boy would have a little color at least, but her prayers hadn't been answered. Master Bryant had told her that if his baby was light, that he would take it into his household as a child of his own. He would then educate him; no one would know that he had black blood in him. She should be grateful, but she wasn't.

Martha tried to keep the master from seeing the baby, but three days afterward the master came to the slave quarters.

"I heard you dropped the sucker," he said. "Why didn't you send word?"

"Well, Massa," she replied, "he turned out real bright. I jus' wanted to keep him for a few mo' days."

"Well," he said, agitated, "bring him to the house tomorrow when you come to work."

The next day Martha brought the baby to the big house. She didn't know where to put him, so she decided to check with the mistress.

Martha had often thought that the mistress and the master had a peculiar marriage. The mistress knew of the master's escapades but made no attempt to stop him from his "activities."

Martha stopped at a door because she heard voices.

"No, Robert Bryant." That was the mistress' voice. "I won't have your bastard in my house! It's bad enough that I don't have any young'uns, but to bring one of your nigra wench's suckers into *my* house. Especially among *my* presence, a high-quality white woman!"

"But Charlotte, the child is almost white! You can't tell that he's got nigra blood. He could be the child we never had. We'll never have a child, because you're barren. You know that!"

"Well, let me see the thang first. I might consider it. Of course, I will have to get a wet nurse for it, and of course, I won't be expected to hold it."

"My dear, you have no choice in the matter. I am your husband, and you will obey me or I will divorce you!" he replied. "I have no intention of giving up my fun just because you don't like it!"

"How dare you talk to me this way, Robert Bryant!" the mistress shouted. "After all I've had to bear with your scandalizing me all over Louisiana, and now this! Well, you're gonna pay for it! I'm gonna order a new wardrobe of twenty dresses, five pairs of underdrawers, ten pairs of gloves, and five pairs of shoes! I'll be going to New Orleans in the morning! Good day, Mr. Bryant." The mistress stormed out of the room.

"Massa, where do I put the young'un," Martha asked, though she didn't want to disturb him.

"You'll just have to put him wherever you'll be working. Tell Jake to make a cradle for him. Since you're the baby's real mother, I suppose you'll have to wet nurse him. Of course, this means that I won't be visiting you anymore, but you'll still work here."

"Thank you, Massa. I sho' do thank you."

"You'll have to keep him for a little while until some house nigras can fix a room up. Meantime you must bring the young'un and nurse when you have time."

"Yessuh, Massa," replied Martha, becoming submissive as she always did within Bryant's presence. "Could I maybe get some food from Aunty Thelma? I been feeling po'ly and I need something extra so the baby can nurse good."

"Well, maybe," the master said, becoming gruff, "but

don't expect no special favors, just 'cause you and me used to be friendly!'' With that he walked away.

MARTHA WAS EIGHTEEN YEARS OLD. HER AND BRYANT HAD been ''friendly'' for about seven months.

A year or so ago, he had badgered her for three months, until finally he had threatened her with a whipping. Martha, being a proud girl, had still refused. Master Bryant's anger got to the boiling point, until finally he whipped her at intervals for three consecutive days. He never stopped from sunup to sundown, until finally Martha relinquished. The alliance had gone on for seven months. Even when Martha got pregnant, the master persisted until she started showing. Then he was suddenly repulsed by her.

Martha was a beautiful girl. She had jet black skin, which

was velvety. Her nose was straight, though it widened at the end. Her face was oval, with arched eyebrows. She had a prettily shaped mouth with thick lips. She had a tiny waist with wide hips. She carried herself proud and tall with all of her five feet, eight inches. Her greatest wish was that someday all of her people would be free.

Martha vehemently hated all white people. She believed that all white people were unintelligent. The reason for this was that white people never saw through the armor of blacks. Blacks could smile graciously in the faces of whites and could plan to poison them when they were alone; in fact they *did* poison them. Martha hated and scorned blacks who *really* meant all that nonsense about bowing and scraping. Black folk in these times have to bow and scrape as long as they don't really mean it, Martha had always thought.

Martha had been brought up with Master Bryant. He was only six years older than she. They had been born about ten years before the nineteenth century. America had just been started back then.

When Martha had listened to the stories of the revolution from the old folk, she felt like laughing. White folk, she had thought, what they know 'bout wanting to be free? Whites really didn't know what it was like to be enslaved, so why did they shout about having liberty? They took others' liberty.

Interlude

Graves of My Grandparents
MARGIE O'BRIEN,
BATTERY CREEK HIGH

As I walk to my grandfather's grave
It starts to rain as if God turned on a faucet
In the distance churchbells ring
As if to say, "I'm here!"
Fog rolls in like a steam engine letting out mist
My heart is beating faster, faster
Snakes come close; they hit and make a sound of swords
All of a sudden a figure stands before me
My grandfather slowly sits down
"Leave this place my dear for you have little time"
In a flash he is gone
A jet flies past
I jump and run as fast as my feet can carry me
Somebody's pounding on my head.
I crash to the ground
Doors are closing.

Black Is Beautiful
THOMASINE ROPER, GRADE 6

Black is a beautiful cat
Wandering in the dark
Trying to catch a mouse.
Black is like soul people getting together
And looking all around the world.
Black is the dark clouds at night
With a shiny moon sitting
Like a ball in the sky.
Black is beautiful.

I'm Not a Bench

GREGORY KINCY, GRADE 4

I told my girlfriend to meet me in the park.
She thought I was a bench.
She tried to move me over.
She sat on me like I would sit on another bench.
I yelled because she sat on me.
Then she said, "Oh, I thought you was a bench."
I'm not even long enough to be a bench.
I don't even have arms like a bench.
How could you think I was a bench?
"I wasn't thinking about you," she said,
"I was thinking about me."
Is that all you do, just think about yourself?
Okay, if that's the way you want it,
I won't come back.
That's the way it is sometimes.

FIFTEEN

Living with Day Care

CHRIS MAYFIELD

I HAVE JUST TAKEN MY four-year-old daughter Mary to her summer morning day camp. She stands, still tense, clutching her lunch box and waving at me like a windmill. "Good-bye, Mama. Good-bye, good-bye!" With my six-month-old second daughter Eliza strapped into her red Snugli pack on my chest, I walk the remaining seven blocks to my office, where I'll hope to cajole her into taking a long morning nap while I proof articles and answer the mail.

Mine and my daughters' attitudes toward day care—our hopes and fears, our gratitude and resentment—are contemporary manifestations of the ways Southern working parents and children have felt for years. Traditionally, Southern working mothers, like others around the nation, have either taken their children to work with them—in the fields, to their employers' houses, even to the floors of the textile mills—or else left them with relatives or friends or older children. Sometimes they've had no choice but to leave them to fend for themselves. And the same attitudes—fear of surrendering individual rights, racism, resentment of big government —which have caused white Southerners to lag behind the rest of the nation in accepting other public, government-controlled institutions have carried over into their attitudes toward day care.

In Northern cities, philanthropic efforts toward caring for needy children date from the day nursery movement in the early 1800s. The Boston Infant School is generally recognized as the first day nursery in America. Opened in 1828, it had as its purpose to "relieve mothers of a part of their domestic care [and] enable them to seek employment," as well as to remove children "from the unhappy association of want and vice" and to place them "under better influences." Almost all early American experiments in day care had as their main intent, not to provide a service along lines set forth by the families themselves, nor simply to extend the family's own nurturance, but rather to salvage the unfortunate children of the lower classes from the supposed inadequacies of their own homes. This "benevolent" intent—the rich and enlightened reaching down to rescue the children of the poor—has characterized much of day-care policy in America since that time.

In the South, however, the first attempts at institutional day care focused on neither the children nor the mothers. Day nurseries established here as part of the WPA program during the Depression functioned primarily to provide jobs for unemployed teachers rather than to uplift the children, though a secondary purpose was to give the children at least one meal a day. During World War II, some WPA day nurseries continued to function, (using funds provided through the Lanham Act of 1942), caring for children while their mothers went to work to keep the nation's industrial and defense machine going in the absence of the men. But this investment in day care was intended merely as a temporary measure, to be discontinued as soon as the soldiers came home from the war and the mothers returned to their homes.

After World War II, many mothers, including an increasing number from the middle class, found that they enjoyed their jobs; others continued to need to work in order to support their families. Between 1948 and 1958, the number of American working women with children under eighteen rose from 20 to 30 percent. But with Lanham funds all withdrawn in early 1946, little group day care was available (only 4 percent of the child-care arrangements reported by working mothers in 1958). Most working mothers kept on making their own largely informal arrangements for the care of their children. Most Americans —especially in the South—still viewed day-care centers with the same contempt or condescension as they looked at other institutional services for families. Day care continued to operate as a last resort for children whose families had failed them.

The postwar aversion to public day care drew strength from a number of 1950s studies centering on a phenomenon known as "maternal deprivation." These studies focused on children (mostly in hospitals or orphanages) who suffered early and prolonged separation from their mothers; the children generally showed evidence of retarded growth and development which sometimes even resulted in death. John Bowlby's influential book *Maternal Deprivation and Mental Health,* published in 1951, explained the situation this way:

What is believed to be essential for mental health is that the infant and young child should experience a warm, intimate and continuous relationship with his mother (or permanent mother substitute) in which both find satisfaction and enjoyment. . . . It is this complex, rich and rewarding relationship with the mother in the early years, varied in countless ways by relations with the father and with siblings, that child psychiatrists and many others now believe to underlie the development of character and mental health.

Bowlby and others helped to reinforce the American enshrinement of the ideal of the nuclear family, in which the father held down a job, the mother worked in the home, and the children remained directly under her wing. These studies also made almost taboo the subject of day care for babies.

I WAS A SMALL CHILD DURING THE EARLY 1950S (BORN THE year Bowlby's book came out) and lived most of my preschool years near my grandparents' farm in southwest Georgia. Like most Southern children of that period (especially in rural areas, where public kindergarten was not yet established), I encountered my first group-care situation in the first grade. The crowds of children, the incomprehensible routine of events, the playground hubbub, the teacher flashing vocabulary cards from her enthronement at the desk, all came as a shocking contrast to my life on the farm, where my father farmed shade tobacco and my mother took care of the kids. In my memory those preschool days have a placid sun-lit quality. I followed Daddy around the hog parlor dressed in overalls just like his; all by myself I walked down the dirt road to church carrying my pink organdy parasol over my head.

My mother's memories of those years are not so bright; caring for three preschoolers, including one colicky baby, is a tough job even with the support of an extended family network such as we enjoyed then. The black families on my grandfather's farm took their children to the fields with them or left them with a relative or older child at home. I visited relatives a lot; once or twice I went to Vacation Bible School with my cousin and had a big time stringing "beads" of colored macaroni. Only the fifth and youngest child in my family went to kindergarten, and that was many years later.

DAY CARE AS A SOCIAL ISSUE IN THE SOUTH WAS FIRST discussed publicly during the early 1960s, in the wake of a new national consciousness about the realities of poverty and injustice. Several new studies asserted that perhaps the mother-child bonds were not so fragile—or even so important—as had been thought; even the taboos against infant day care started to lift. Day-care centers became "child development" centers and were given the responsibility of educating the child intellectually as well as of protecting his or her physical safety. In addition, the idea that women—even mothers—should have the right to help support their families began to seem less outrageous. The reality is, of course, that poor mothers, black and white, have always worked to support their families with or without the aid of an extended network of relatives and friends.

In 1964, my father was a young Episcopal priest pioneering in an inner-city church in Jacksonville, Florida. His church, St. Mary's, was in a classic "transitional" neighborhood, called Springfield. Once fashionable and even wealthy, Springfield's big old Victorian houses were now mostly split up into apartments, but the cracked pavingstone sidewalks were still shaded by live oaks and chinaberry trees and banked with overgrown azaleas. The population—except for a few tough widows hanging onto their homeplaces—consisted mostly of young white families come into the city from the impoverished north Florida countryside in search of jobs. Many were supported only by the mother. If a parent were lucky enough to find a job at all, it did not pay enough for the family to hire a baby-sitter, and generally the supporting network of grandmas and aunts had been left behind in the country. If nobody in the family could find a job, they could sometimes get onto welfare, but the welfare payments— around $97 a month for a family of four—were hardly enough to pay for rent and utilities; feeding the kids was usually a real challenge.

Not surprisingly, Daddy saw the establishment of a day-care center as one of the first tasks that the church in this neighborhood must undertake. It was not easy, however, to convince the congregation of this imperative. At that time (but not for long, under Daddy's tenure), St. Mary's was still made up mostly of well-to-do suburban families. They had grown up in Springfield and wanted to maintain their ties to the old church. They might easily have supported a church kindergarten program, a sort of extended Sunday school, with a hefty tuition and a few scholarships for deserving neighborhood kids.

But the community needed a full day-care program— with fees charged on a sliding scale—serving infants through five-year-olds, with an after-school program for older kids. The day-care center would also need to be integrated, since (this was 1964) a few black families were moving into the neighborhood.

After months of long and heated discussion, the argument was finally clinched when three-year-old Denise (whose mother worked nights as a waitress) wandered into a vestry meeting one night from her apartment down the street, where she had gotten lonely all by herself. In her nightgown, with her pale pinched little face and big blue eyes, she presented irrefutable (and appealing) proof of the plight of Springfield's small children.

THE EPISCOPAL CHILD DEVELOPMENT CENTER OPENED IN the fall of 1964, in the old rectory next to the church. Enrollment got off to a slow start—16 kids the first day, with eight teachers. Five years later the center was literally bursting at its seams, serving over 100 kids. The center received no federal funds; the church subsidized it with about half the operating costs.

I began working at the Episcopal center the fall it opened (at age fourteen), after school for two hours each day and full time during the summer. After the initial slow start, we never had enough staff; though a core group of staff members worked there the whole five years, many of the staff, like the children, and like Springfield people in general, came and left with staggering speed and suddenness. And though the staff had many strengths (much warmth and talent), there were also exasperating weaknesses. Several women, towers of strength in the center when sober, periodically came to work drunk. The staff often seemed to be adrift in a boiling sea of children. Many a time I was left in charge of thirty children on the playground, for a couple of hours at a time. This complex combination of assets and liabilities often created struggles between the management (my father and a succession of directors) and the workers.

In the center's early days—the first year mainly—we contended with the threat of physical danger as well: bomb threats, ugly phone calls, arson scares. No violence actually occurred, and gradually we stopped having the kids rehearse what to do in case a Molotov cocktail came through the window (prone on floor, hands clasped behind

head). We attributed these threats mainly to the fact that
the center was increasingly integrated. My father and the
center were regularly denounced in the local right-wing
scandal sheet.

On the other hand, life at the Springfield center fairly
snapped with vitality. There was a great deal of singing and
storytelling. One teacher regularly took her group of
three-year-olds outside for large-scale fingerpainting
sessions, hosing off both the sidewalk and the kids
afterward. Most of the grass on the playground was
trampled off, but this left plenty of dirt for our elaborate
mud-pie sculptures.

Something I *don't* remember about those years was any
doubt in our minds—mine, my family's, the staff's—that
despite a few lapses, like temporarily losing track of a kid,
the center was a better place for most of these kids to be
during the day than their own homes were, whether a
parent was at home or not. Even the hostile church
members didn't question the idea that we could do a better
job than most of "those mothers." The main challenge we
saw was how to avoid turning kids away for lack of space
or staff. It's hard to argue in favor of preschoolers being left
locked in dark, cold apartments alone all day, as many of

ours were before they came to the center. One five-year-old girl we knew had already learned how to cut up and cook a chicken! But looking back, what we offered instead does not always appear to have been measurably more wholesome. At its best, the center was a bright and sheltering place where the children could play and rest and even learn; at its worst, it became a kind of no-man's-land —crowded, noisy, aimless, and confused. The demand for day care was large, but our resources and experience could not come close to keeping up.

MY FAMILY LEFT JACKSONVILLE IN THE SUMMER OF 1969 and headed back to our native Georgia countryside, to the small (population 7,000) town of Swainsboro. Here again, the community's need and desire for day care soon surfaced despite the existence of the traditional small-town/rural nurturing network of relatives and neighbors. Again, my father and a community group faced opposition from certain powers within the town: finding someone to rent them a building to house the center was difficult, and securing the $5,000 needed as local seed money for Title XX funding took months. But the national belief in the efficacy and importance of preschool education was filtering down into the hinterlands of the South. Nationally, at this point, the women's movement had reinforced the belief born in the 1960s that day care could be a great force for social equality, enlarging the world of the child while at the same time freeing the mother from the bondage of the hearth. Many Swainsboro parents eagerly awaited a center which would provide not only safety and an educational program for their children but also freedom for the mother.

The Swainsboro center—like the one in Springfield but with greatly improved facilities—quickly grew to seam-bursting size. This center was fully integrated. The children's parents generally worked in the local textile mill or the plastics factory, where wages for the women started at about $1.75 an hour (and never got much higher). Like the Springfield center, this one unquestionably provided a

service which many parents deemed better than the
alternatives. The board of directors included many parents,
but for the most part their involvement had little impact on
the center's operation, as parents were often too timid or
uncertain of what they wanted to speak out on regarding
vital issues. The center was closed once or twice in 1980
because of mismanagement; at last report it was closed, but
a group of parents was trying to reopen it.

The staff-child ratio was generally better in the
Swainsboro than in the Springfield center. Yet staff morale
was chronically low. The center's leadership, while
intelligent and well meaning, generally failed to exert much
energy in the shaping of the center's program or to inspire
the staff with a sense of mission. As a result, many staff
members viewed their work (naturally enough) simply as
another low-paying job, and consequently the children
received essentially custodial care.

When I worked there, the situation was especially rough
in the Toddler House. Toddlers are notoriously hard to deal
with. Compared to babies, they're big and messy and
unruly; compared to older kids, they're still not toilet
trained, can't talk very well, and require constant
supervision. They're also especially sensitive to change, and
most child psychologists say that separation from parents is
particularly upsetting during this period—from fifteen
months to about two-and-a-half years. This is also an age
when most children are not greatly interested in their peers
and do not have much success in playing cooperatively.
Instead, the fascinating world of the grownups draws their
attention.

The Toddler House in Swainsboro offered little to
compensate the toddler for the difficult separation from
home and parents. Although kindly and well-meaning, staff
members for the most part lacked the energy to play much
with the children. The kids milled around the several
crowded rooms, knocking into one another, whining, or
sucking on their pacifiers with the introverted vacancy of a
group of opium eaters. I substituted there for two weeks
one summer and found it one of the grimmest episodes in
my day-care career.

Every hour or two, the children's diapers were all

changed—a horrifying ritual. Each staff member had one
rag and a pail of water, and we would move around the
rooms like cow punchers through a cattle yard, corraling
children and pinning them down then and there on the
floor. The one rag was used to wipe all the six or seven
bottoms that fell to each person's portion. To my
consternation, one lady assiduously wiped the juice and
crackers off their faces with that same rag. I reported this
practice to the director but later heard that it was still in use.

Since it took a fair amount of time and energy to get all
the toddlers' shoes on, they didn't go outside much even in
good weather, and hardly at all in the winter. Once they
were out, the staff took this opportunity for a much-needed
break; they sat relaxing by the side of the building and left
the children to their own devices. Since I was just there as
a substitute, and was also a good twenty years younger
than most of the regular staff, I had a little more energy to
devote to the kids. It didn't take much. The slightest
overture brought an unexpected and overwhelming
response, all out of proportion to the effort. I picked up a
plastic telephone receiver that was lying in the grass and
handed it to one of the kids, holding an invisible receiver
to my own ear. "Hello. Is Pee Wee there?" Pee Wee,
almost inaudibly, but grinning from ear to ear, answered,
"Yeah." "Well, hey, Pee Wee, how you doing." (Long
pause, heavy breathing.) "Bye." I looked up to see at least
ten other toddlers lined up for their turn to enact this
dialogue. And so it went for the next hour and a half, while
the regular staff eyed us coldly from the sidelines.

But who can blame them? One toddler alone is enough
to drive his or her own parents up the wall on occasion.
These day-care workers had to contend with a whole
houseful of toddlers at their worst: frightened, whiny,
confused and demanding. For a wage of around $2 an
hour, who could reasonably expect anything better, day
after day?

THE MOST OBVIOUS PROBLEM WITH THE SPRINGFIELD AND
Swainsboro day-care centers was simply that the need was
too great, that they took on too much, with too few

resources. Although the directors at both centers were compassionate and knowledgeable, they often shied away from making the difficult decisions to dismiss an incompetent employee or turn away a needy child for lack of space. Suppose a center were run by a group of early-childhood specialists and staffed with people carefully chosen by them. Suppose it were well funded and observed the recommended staff-child ratios, strictly limiting its enrollment to what it could handle. Under these circumstances, might not the center provide care for children which would actually reinforce rather than cripple healthy development?

I thought my chance had come to test this hypothesis soon after I graduated from college, when I landed a job supervising three-year-olds in the highly rated Durham Nursery Schools Association, a nonprofit, United Fund-supported chain of day-care centers at four locations in Durham, North Carolina. (This number has since grown to six.) Although located on the leafy-green outskirts of town, the center I worked at nevertheless served children from all over Durham, with the association providing bus service for children who needed it.

The lead teacher in charge of the center was extremely competent and well organized. The rooms were bright and neatly arranged, the playground shady and well equipped. When I arrived, the children were actually outside enjoying themselves. Best of all, the center was small; licensed for forty kids, forty was all it had, ages three to five. The black kids to white kids ratio was about 40 to 60. About a third were subsidized by Social Services; the fees were arranged on a sliding scale, peaking at $21 a week.

The morning program was highly structured, and closely supervised by the lead teacher. The schedule called for a storytelling session and an hour and a half of supervised activities (painting, block building, cookie making). The atmosphere would ideally be one of subdued excitement as the children worked together harmoniously at their chosen tasks, while the aides and I moved unobtrusively from group to group, providing guidance and stimulation. I was to draw up a lesson plan for every week (birds, trains, community helpers) and was responsible for involving my aides as creatively as possible in the planning and execution of the lessons.

About 10:30, the children cleaned up the rooms and went outside to play until time to wash up for lunch, which was served around 12:00. Then followed naptime; then the afternoon program, for which I was solely responsible since the lead teacher left at 3:00. This was supposed to be a modified, more relaxed version of the morning program; it didn't have to have a weekly motif, but I was expected to have ready at least two activities for the children to choose from, in addition to free play on the playground. We made paper masks and telephone wire jewelry and painted long swaths of paper taped to the fence. Another activity that I initiated—and that I still feel more proud of than anything else I accomplished that year—was making big newsprint "books." A group of us would gather on the sidewalk with our book and bunch of crayons; each child would have a turn to dictate a story to me and then illustrate it. The narrative skills of even the youngest children developed greatly over the months; they also took a lively interest in each other's work. Some of the wilder tales became general favorites, read over and over again, not only by me, but by the other staff members as well, to an enthralled audience.

It took quite a while, however, before I measured up to the requirements of the morning program. I wasn't used to being supervised and had never had to fit into a pre-existing structure. At other centers, I simply fended for myself and my kids the best I could; nobody paid much attention to what I did, so long as the kids didn't tear down the walls or kill each other. But here the lead teacher stood discreetly in the doorway during circle time to observe my rendition of *Little Cabin in the Woods*. After a month she gave me a formal evaluation in which she awarded me a "5" (out of five) for warmth and positive attitude, but only a "2" for discipline; my lesson plans rated a dismal "1." Weeks passed before I didn't spend 90 percent of circle time yelling at the kids to be quiet. And I never got over feeling uncomfortable about telling my aides what to do. It seemed to me that they were every bit as smart and certainly worked at least as hard as I did, yet I was painfully conscious of the discrepancy between their paychecks and mine.

We all worked hard and tried to do everything we were supposed to do. We had regular staff meetings, parent conferences, covered-dish suppers. We could refer the most troubled children to a child psychiatry clinic. We had plenty of money for supplies; if you went into the supply closet and found only a half-empty jar of white paint, you blamed yourself for not having done the paperwork necessary to order more. A long list of substitutes could be called to replace a sick staff member, and rarely (and only temporarily) were the recommended staff-child ratios violated.

Yet after one year—almost to the day—I resigned, completely exhausted in body and spirit, and seriously and lastingly discouraged about the possibilities of good center day care. And I was not an isolated instance. The composition of the staff changed almost completely during the year I was there. The average child stayed in the center much longer than the average staff person. What was wrong?

Two central factors together can doom the most professional, best-equipped, most well-meaning day-care enterprise. One is the long, long center day. This is of course an insuperable problem for children whose parents must work full time. But it greatly strains a young child's tolerance for separation from his or her home and parents. Selma Fraiberg, professor of child psychoanalysis at the University of Michigan and director of the university's Child Development Project, describes the shortcomings of even supposedly ideal day-care programs in her book *Every Child's Birthright: In Defense of Mothering:*

When pre-school children are separated from their mothers for nine to ten hours there is a point of diminishing returns in the nursery day, and finally a point where no educational benefits accrue to the child. By afternoon, after naptime, restlessness, tearfulness, whininess or lassitude become epidemic in the group of

*three- to six-year-olds. Even the most expert teachers
have difficulty sustaining the program and restoring
harmony. What we see is longing for mother and home.
The nice teacher, the "best friends," the lovely toys can
no longer substitute.*

This was certainly true of our "ideal" center. It was the
long two and a half hours after naptime which did
everybody in. No matter how nice we tried to be to the
children, and how much they liked us, the center was still
not home and they could never completely relax.

And we were by no means always so nice. Day care is
very, very hard work; even in the best center, with
reasonable staff-child ratios like ours, children demand a
huge amount of attention and patience and physical care.
As the day wears on, they often become noisy, whiny,
quarrelsome, and destructive. On rainy days, when there's
not even the relief of going outside, the tension can grow
almost murderous between the grown-ups and the kids
locked up together in the same old rooms hour after hour.
I have a persistent image of myself sitting on the floor
trying to read a story, the children crawling all over me,
coughing in my face with their inevitable day-care colds. I
clench my fists to keep from brushing them off like
troublesome mosquitoes. The parents—and the outside
world in general, including the administrators of Durham
Nursery Schools Association, in their remote East Durham
office—simply did not know how it was, for us and for the
kids, day after long day, week after week. Parents had no
say in—were not even informed about—vital issues
affecting the day care their children received: how much
the staff was paid, how the program was structured or
why, what the rules and regulations were. At the parent
conferences, we discussed how their child fit into our
program and what they could do at home to aid his or her
adjustment. We talked very little about what should be
altered in the program; there wasn't much point, since all
was ordained from above.

And herein lies the second central flaw in our center:
Durham Nursery Schools Association was not set up or
governed by the people (besides the kids) most closely

affected—the parents and the staff. The administrators of Durham Nursery Schools were, and I'm sure still are, well-meaning and professionally competent people; the association's centers are indubitably far better than average. But professional competence *and* strong family and community involvement are both essential to the operation of a truly satisfactory day-care center.

The unhappiness of oppressed workers is another timeworn but accurate theme. Admittedly, day-care workers are less oppressed than many others. The pay is notoriously bad, but at least the work is interesting and not usually physically hazardous (unless you count the dangers of catching every sore throat or stomach bug that sweeps the center, as I did that year). But when day-care workers are overworked and underpaid, their unhappiness directly and crucially affects the well-being of an even more vulnerable group of people—the children. Professional opinion is unanimous on one aspect of day care: rapid staff turnover is not good for the children. The miraculous and saving factor is that many day-care workers, regardless of the low pay and demanding and responsible work, do put forth the terrific amount of energy required to do a good job in day care. But their dedication is taken for granted rather than rewarded, except by the love and the healthy development of the children they serve. And the children, of course, do not sit on the board of directors and do not allocate funds nor set wage guidelines.

Another major flaw was an arbitrarily hierarchical structure within the center itself. As I saw it, the "teachers" and the "aides" all worked equally hard and all (regardless of education or expertise) bore equally great responsibility for the welfare of the kids. Therefore, they ought to have been paid equally and to have shared equally in decision making and program planning, along lines agreed upon by parents and staff and, ideally, supported by visiting experts and frequent workshops. In our center, although I was theoretically supposed to "work closely with" my aides and "involve them in the lesson plans," in reality I found the difference in our wages and our prestige to be an insuperable barrier to true cooperation.

During the latter part of the year that I worked for Durham Nursery Schools, tumult did arise among the workers. Led by one aide from our center—a person exceptionally devoted to the kids and beloved by them— staff from all four centers met among ourselves several times and presented a list of demands to the director and a meeting of the board of directors. These included:

—wage increases (the aides made a little less than the federal minimum wage and didn't feel that the privilege of wolfing down their lunch with the kids made up the difference);
—election of workers and parents to an advisory board which would meet with the director about policy issues concerning the centers;
—overtime pay rather than compensatory leave for extra hours worked (since leave time often left the centers understaffed);
—reduction of the paperwork load for lead teachers;
—elimination of the nine-hour workday;
—exploration of allowing more people to work part-time shifts (one six-hour shift was already allocated to each center) to cut down on staff burnout and consequently reduce staff turnover;
—toothbrushes for the kids, since the centers' menus were highly starchy and sugary; association officials claimed that they could not sustain this expense, though they had just hired their third highly paid administrator;
—the hiring of teenagers to help with the exhausting afternoon program.

Despite the fact that many parents vocally backed up these demands, the director and the board made no concessions at all. The demands themselves were branded as personal attacks on the director and as being selfish and inconsiderate of the children. One board member, a high-ranking officer of a local bank, offered us this advice: "If you can't get along on the wages we pay, maybe you should go over to Durham Tech and take a course in budget management!"

Shortly afterward, I gave my month's notice.

TODAY I'M ATTEMPTING TO MEET WHAT SEEMS TO MOST
people (me too sometimes) the outrageous challenge of
trying to combine a full-time job with the care of my two
young daughters—*without* resorting to full-time day care
for either one. Mary, age four, goes to preschool from 9:00
to 12:00 every weekday morning, and she loves it; in the
afternoons, she either comes over to my office and plays in
the kids' room provided at work or, more often, goes home
with either me or her father, depending on our work
schedules for that day. Even in this situation, separation
from Mama is still somewhat of a big deal for her. No
matter how much she looks forward to the day's events
and her wonderful, exciting world of school, she is very
conscious of the fact that she's going to school while I'm
going to work; many times I can see her swallowing a lump
in her throat. She then goes on to have a fine morning.

And I'm anachronistic enough to feel that her reactions
are healthy. I value intense attachment, deep feelings, acute
sensibility. I'm glad that she loves her school, too, but I
wouldn't want her to stay there all day—no matter *how*
wonderful it was—to be endlessly entertained, interminably
amused. The director of an excellent small day-care center
in Georgia said to me once that the single element she feels
children miss out on in day care is solitude—not the
terrifying loneliness of being lost in a crowded institution,
but the creative solitude of playing independently, with a
protective adult within call. Children need time, as this
director put it, for "swinging on the garden gate," for
simply staring out into space and experiencing what it's like
to be alone, with nothing in particular to do. I want my
kids to learn to play by themselves, and this is one strength
that they are not likely to gain at a day-care center.

My six-month-old baby Eliza I keep with me all the time.
In another six months I may consider a good part-time
day-care home. She has a crib in my office, and I'm lucky
enough to work with people who tolerate not only her
presence when she's quiet but also her occasional
screaming and the way she can dominate a conversation;
some of them even seem to enjoy her company. I'm also
lucky to have flexible working hours; very few parents do.
Fewer still enjoy my ability to work a lot at home. In

addition, I have a husband whose job allows him to shoulder his part of the child-care burdens. Even with all these advantages, many women I know still feel I'm "sacrificing myself." I sense (and this does show something about how attitudes toward child-rearing have changed in the South, at least among a certain percentage of the population) that *any* reservations about day care—let alone the decision not to use it at all—are regarded as somewhat reactionary. The fact that Eliza refuses to take a bottle at all, and thus in fact can't be separated from her food source (i.e., me), is seen as very unfortunate for me and certainly eccentric on her part.

WORKING WITHOUT DAY CARE IS CERTAINLY NO PICNIC but knowing what I know about the realities of day care *as it currently exists,* I feel the challenges I've chosen are worthwhile. But what about all the parents to whom even my child-care arrangements are a luxury? What about working mothers with no husbands, or families in which both parents work inflexible hours at a factory that doesn't want kids around?

I can readily conceive of a day-care system with which even I could be comfortable. The key as I see it is a combination of strong professional leadership and energetic community control. The Swainsboro center and the Durham association demonstrate the pitfalls that can open up when power is allocated solely to a tough-minded director or to an unmotivated group of parents and workers. Ideally, the two parties would struggle together to hammer out a program both professionally sound and sensitive to the needs of the particular families involved. Some of the issues that would arise are questions of part-time or full-time care, type of discipline used, whether the emphasis would be on school readiness or on cooperative playing. The parents' involvement is crucial because it is very important that a child feel that the day-care environment is a real extension of his or her family into the community—rather than a corrective applied to negate the family's influence, as is too often the case with day care for the poor. Only under these

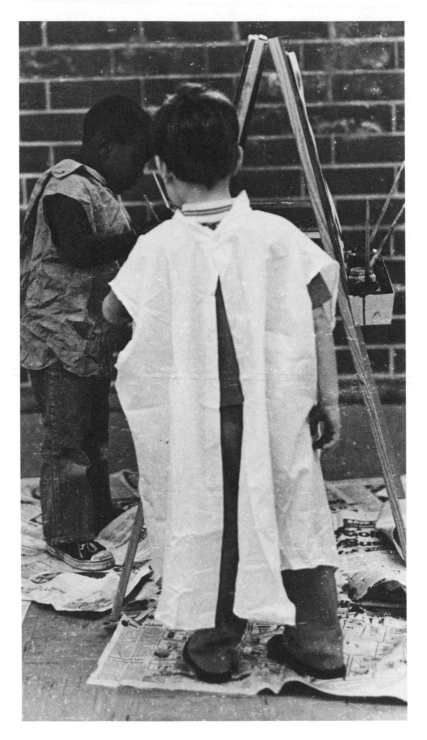

circumstances will the child feel secure enough to put down the deep roots that every child needs in order to love and be loved.

Speaking as a veteran day-care worker, day-care mother and working parent, this is how I would envision the ideal day-care system.

Crucial to the success of this program would be the emphasis on day-care "systems" rather than just centers. Centers should not be the only model or option for day care. They can work well, especially for older kids, and especially if half-day use is encouraged for as many parents as can manage it. But as Margaret Steinfels points out in *Who's Minding the Children?* (1972), "Emphasis on centers alone may . . . freeze day care into rigid patterns, reinforce our tendency to always depend on institutional solutions and satisfy an 'edifice complex.' " She recommends instead—as have many other educators and child development specialists, including Kenneth Kenniston, Selma Fraiberg, and Sally Provence—a nucleus of day-care services. A day-care center could serve its traditional functions while, in addition, providing after-school care for older children (as both the Springfield and the Swainsboro centers did). It could serve also as an information exchange center, encouraging parents to share child-care services as much as possible. The center could coordinate and supervise the informal network of day-care home operators and could even function as a kind of home base for them, where they could come to observe methods of dealing with a particular age or type of child or where they could bring their groups of children periodically for a story hour or a dance lesson. The center could encourage retired people in the community to become more involved with their younger neighbors by working a few hours a week in the center (as one retired couple did at the Durham center) or by keeping, say, one baby in their home part-time. In essence, such a day-care system would help to create the connections necessary for meaningful community control. Families would be enabled to extend themselves further into the community while at the same time to assert more control over their own lives. This involvement could be as valuable in a dreary suburb as in an urban ghetto.

The need for day care must be publicly acknowledged and supported with much more government money. To develop a day-care system, a day-care council would be set up in every city or town or rural county. (Such a project was recently refused funding by the Durham city council.) This council would encourage neighborhoods to set up their own day-care systems, and would provide high-quality professional input into the organization and operation of the centers. The councils would then inspect, license and fund the systems. The important criteria for licensing would be the physical and psychological safety of the children and the integral role of the parents and the community in planning and operating the system. Parents at factories and other workplaces should also be encouraged and helped to set up day-care arrangements near their work sites, where they could visit with their children during breaks.

Within the system itself, particularly in the centers, the reality that all care-givers are equally important to the children would be reflected in pay and hierarchy arrangements. In recognition of the value of the job, day-care workers would be well paid. They would also be recruited as much as possible from within the community itself. This would evolve as a natural process, since the center would be operated by the neighborhood. Parents and staff together would determine how the center would be run and would inspire each other with the sense of commitment necessary to a nurturing child-care situation.

Provision should be made for paid leaves of absence running for several months and coming up every three or four years. In addition to respite and rejuvenation, this arrangement would also allow workers to take courses in child development, dance, art, children's literature— enrichment which would then be brought back into the day-care experience for the children. This kind of self-improvement is expected of day-care workers now, but considering the exhausting, unrelenting pace they keep up, few have much energy or time left for such projects.

Furthermore, day care must no longer be viewed by politicians as the solution for getting "freeloaders" off the welfare rolls. Poor and single parents should be able to decide for themselves if they want to work outside their homes and place their children in day care, or if they want to stay home and do the important work of raising children. Right now we have the opposite situation. As Steinfels points out: "Throughout its history, day care has been linked with welfare and social deviancy. In our society, services thus linked are almost inevitably substandard." In *All Our Children,* Kenneth Kenniston proposes in detail a program of negative income tax and guaranteed income, which would, among other things, allow all families to make basic choices about the arrangement of their working lives.

We are nearing a point where over half the mothers in this country will be in the workforce; right now, 6.4 million preschool children (38 percent) have working mothers. In the South, this trend is accelerating even more rapidly than in the nation as a whole. Day care as a reality, and as an economic necessity for many families, is obviously here to stay. But its shape, and consequently the condition of our children and the future of our society, has yet to be given serious and methodical consideration by most Americans, or by our government.

SOURCES

Fraiberg, Selma. *Every Child's Birthright: In Defense of Mothering.* New York: Basic Books, 1977.

Keniston, Kenneth and the Carnegie Council on Children. *All Our Children: The American Family Under Pressure.* New York: Harcourt, Brace, Jovanovich, 1972.

Keyserling, Mary Dublin. *Windows on Day Care.* New York: National Council of Jewish Women, 1972.

Provence, Sally A. *The Challenge of Day Care.* New Haven: Yale University Press, 1977.

Steinfels, Margaret O. *Who's Minding the Children?* New York: Simon and Schuster, 1973.

SIXTEEN

A Visit to the White House

MICHAEL BERT MCCARTHY

IT WAS TYPICAL OF Southern jails in the 1950s: a concrete and brick, two-story building with the first floor housing the sheriff's offices, jail booking office, and small kitchen; the second floor, a hollow shell with a steel-barred cage set about four feet from the surrounding green walls and three feet below the dimly lit ceiling. There were segregated cells, each with two flat, metal-slatted bunks and an encrusted toilet bowl-wash basin combination. The floor, an unpainted, gray-grouted cement, sloped toward drain holes to facilitate a monthly hosing and to accommodate the inevitable flooding by a rampaging prisoner.

The two fifteen-year-old boys occupying the front cells by the security door were typical, too—except they were clothed in state-issued, white cotton boxer shorts, dirty with road clay, torn by briars and thistles. They were runaways from what was called, by some, the Florida School for Boys, and by others, the Florida Industrial School at Marianna. Whatever. It all meant the same thing in the end. They were juvenile escapees from Florida's one reform school for boys. And that's why both boys had that look of cold, infantilizing terror about them. They knew what awaited runaways.

At a little past three o'clock in the afternoon, the security door swung open, and the county jailer came in, dressed

122

in the gaudy green, gray, and gold patch uniform, keys clanking and clinking against the hollow silence. Then came the two state men in the dress of the boys' school informality: white solid or thin-striped, short-sleeved shirts; brown or black slacks; white cotton or black argyle socks; black or brown laced shoes. These were the men with taut grins and white Baptist faces, men off the broken farms of north Florida, southern Georgia and Alabama, men in the benevolent tradition of the Southern paternal order. Hard Christian men serving the state, steeped in the doctrine of original sin and the swift application of salvation and retribution.

The jailer keyed the lock and told the boys in a not unkindly way to back up against the cell door with their hands behind them. A state man manacled first one, then the other boy. He asked each if the cuffs were too tight; they in turn mumbled their no's. They were motioned out of the cell—the slimmer of the two, Mike, moving lamely on his left leg. His knee, ankle, and foot were encrusted with blood and dirt.

The jailer led them down the hollow concrete steps, into the booking room, and the state men motioned the boys to the wooden bench by the wall as they signed them out. The officials exchanged their good-byes, then the boys were led squinting into the orange-white sun of the parking lot. The omnipresent grey state car sat waiting, a well-used transport for state supplies and runaway boys.

The state car headed northwest out of Apalachicola on Highway 98; the boys were seated in the rear, the window and door handles removed. Fifty miles per hour along the golden Gulf Coast, where the sun splashed on white beaches, green-brown saw grass, the sparse northern Florida pines. Then north on 71 out of Port St. Joe, through Wewahitchka, along the Dead Lake.

Little was said. What was there to say? They were taking them back to Marianna. Going to Hell in the "Sunshine State" of Yankee tourists and retirees.

The state car moved along the three-hour trip through the small towns of Blountsville and Altha, through the open grazing land of the humid Florida panhandle. The road signs marked the distance as they drew nearer and nearer to Marianna. At the twenty-mile sign, cold sweat began to film on the bottom of the boys' feet, in the palms of their hands, in their armpits; it trickled through the hair of their groins, down and around their testicles to the vinyl seats, soaking their asses. The near-naked boys sat, manacled arms behind their backs, on the elevated rear seat of the state station wagon, gawked at by pedestrians from curb-sides and passengers in faster vehicles. Images conjured of Southern times past, of other runaways, their black bodies manacled, clothing torn and tattered, seated in the rear of a wagon.

The state car passed through the rock portals and up the road leading to the central offices of the school; it swung left and stopped in front of the director's office. Mr. Dennis, the school's Boy Scout leader, got out of the passenger seat and walked to the office door; he said something to the inside. Then, back at the car, he waited. Soon a tall, angular man, the director, came out. He had a slight, right-legged limp borne with a sternness he seemed to take pride in. He neither looked at nor spoke to the boys but motioned to the driver with a long, gaunt arm, pointing toward the dining room and kitchen, and he said something to Dennis.

Dennis said, "OK," and got back into the car. They drove the short, pine-tree-lined road past the kitchen and stopped before a one-story, white cement, windowless building. "You boys just sit there for a minute." Dragging some keys from his pocket, Dennis unlocked the building's heavy wooden door and disappeared into the darkness. The boys could hear the clamor and din from the dining room as nearly 400 boys sat down to their evening meal.

Shortly, the director appeared at the right side of the car and reached through the front window to unlock the rear door. "You can get out now," he said to Mike. Dennis reappeared through the doorway and opened the car's left rear door, telling the other boy, Woody, to get out. Motioning toward the building, the director said, "You boys get on in there." Dennis led them out of the late afternoon Florida sunlight into the near darkness of the building known as the White House.

The boys were led into a dank, whitewashed corridor six

feet wide, eight feet high. The aged walls were lit only by a single wire-encased bulb glaring against the musty ceiling. Three-quarters of the way down the corridor were two identical rooms, one on either side, both lit with bulbs encased in the rusty wire mesh. The boys were directed to the one on the left—the Colored Boys' Room it was called —equal and identical, separate by law. Word had it the only difference was in the number of strokes given blacks.

The room held nothing but a rusting, GI-green army cot, with an uncovered, striped mattress and pillow, dark with the liquid stains of human misery. The two runaways were uncuffed and ordered to sit on the cot. The two state men stood over them, silent, watching as the terror began to tremble their bodies. A third state man stood waiting in the corridor. The director began to question them: "Why did you boys run? . . . Don't you know you can't get away from here? You boys are lucky; farmers hereabouts shoot runaways. Either that or the swamps get them. What's your excuse? . . . If you've got one, I want to hear it."

Woody began to cry softly, the director's voice signaling the inevitable emotional buildup to the beating. Mike, crying too, tried to speak: "I don't know. . . . I couldn't take anymore. . . . I just wanted to get away. . . . I. . . ." Dennis said nothing; the director slowly tapped his game right foot. Finally, Mike gave up, his head bowed. "All right," the director said. "Which of you will go first?" Neither answered. The director pointed to Mike. "You then, let's go—into the other room." And giving a nod to Dennis, the director led Mike into the White Boys' Room.

Pointing to the army cot, the director gave the instructions: "All right now, son, it'll go easier on you if you do as I tell you. You're to lay down on the cot on your belly; turn your face to the wall. If I were you, I'd stuff the corner of that pillow in your mouth. Once we begin, don't turn your head. Don't cry out or scream. If you do, we start all over again. Place both hands on the cot frame and keep hold of it. Do not try to get up or try to stop us. If you do, we'll send for some kitchen boys to hold you down. I'd try to stay as relaxed as you can; you're less likely to be hurt."

The mask of sternness began to slip. Something—remorse

perhaps—began to flow down the long lines of his face.
"Now get this straight in your head. Every boy is told
about running away. You knew the punishment; you've
seen boys brought back to your cottage from here. You
knew what to expect when you were caught. So you asked
for this."

The new mask melted into place: two hundred years old;
seen from a thousand Protestant pulpits; from a multitude
of Southern court benches at sentencing time; before the
cringing figure of the mischievous child; at the hanging of a
good slave gone bad; before the daughter being sent away
from the unacceptable lover. The patriarch stood towering
before Mike. A long pause followed as he turned the shoe
of his flawed right leg on the cement floor. Then he spoke
the formula: "Let me tell you something, son, this is going
to hurt me more than it will you."

Having said his piece, the director pulled himself erect,
the tone of self-pitying condescension gone from his face:
"All right now, lay on down there, turn your head, and get
ahold of the cot." The boy, visibly shaken, did as he was
told. The director spoke again: "You'd best do as I said
and stick the corner of that pillow in your mouth." Mike
caught the pillow corner in his mouth, turned his head flat
on its side, shut his eyes, and waited. Seconds, minutes of
clenched waiting. His body trembled. Sweat ran under his
arms; sweat ran down the crack of his ass, the
white-cotton shorts turning damp, clinging to the skin of his
buttocks. He lay there in the silence, waiting for it to begin.

He heard Dennis's footsteps return, the director step
halfway out the door and tell him to "hit the fan." And
then he heard the awful roar of the huge exhaust fan at the
corridor's end. The whole of the White House seemed to
shudder under its force. It filled the room until no sound
but the fan was possible.

Half in fear, reacting to the shock of the fan, Mike turned
his head toward the director. In a glimpse of terror, he saw
it. Pushing his head back toward the wall, he took the
pillow again into his mouth; his hands squeezed the bed
frame; he clamped his eyes shut.

The first stroke exploded. The sound like the booming
Ka-Pow of a shotgun slammed into his ears as the impact

of the blow penetrated into the tissues of his ass. The second stroke was higher, cutting just across the top elastic of his shorts. *Crack-Pow.* The boom echoed louder off the barren walls; the shock of pain cracked into his lower back. He was driven deep into the mattress.

The mattress and springs pushed his body up to meet the third stroke: *Crack-Pow.* The skin on the back of his thighs was ripped upward with the stroke's completion. *Crack-Pow.* Two thousand, three thousand, four thousand. . . . The pain began to turn a deep, bright red as it ran through him.

He saw it clearly. Swinging in an arc over the director's head, slapping into the cheeks of his ass.

THE PADDLE. AN INNOCUOUS, SCHOOLROOM TERM GIVEN it by the director. The Paddle. Two strips of quarter-inch polished leather, two feet long, over two inches wide, separated by a sixteenth-inch piece of taut, pliant sheet metal. Attached to a four-inch rounded hand grip, the leather was perforated on either side midway down, with one-eighth-inch holes, ending in a half-inch long taper. The effect brought the whipping weapon down in a cracking slap that drove through the thinness of the cotton shorts, into the upper tissues of the skin. Halfway through the beating, the holes were filled with blood-covered flesh. The paddle began to pull and suck to the side and away. Finally, with each stroke, the tapered end snapped the flesh, cracking it wherever it had grown taut and swollen.

Crack-Pow. The strokes were coming in a marked rhythm now. As the director began each stroke, the foot of his twisted right leg slid on the cement floor, making a terse rasping sound. Then as the paddle was swung up and over the director's head, it scraped against the ceiling just before it came down against the flesh. Between the eighth and twelfth blows the boy, now crying softly into the pillow, began to try different measures to ease the blows. First he waited the split second between the scrape on the ceiling and the impact, tightened his lower back, ass, and legs, and just as the blow landed, he would force himself to go limp.

Between the sixteenth and twentieth, he tried just the opposite. Just as the blow was to land, he would go rigid; as it ended, he went loose.

Somewhere between the twenty-third and twenty-sixth, he succumbed to deep guttural moaning, biting the pillow deeply so it was tight against his tongue and the roof of his mouth. He knew nothing would ease the pain as the director, in his practiced, methodical manner, alternated the strokes first to the middle buttocks, then to the back of the legs, then to the small of the back, then hit just one cheek, the tapered end snatching and tearing at the inside of the crevice.

At the thirty-first stroke, the boy went into a state of semishock. The roar of the fan, the lunging breathing of the director, the scraping foot, the paddle catching at the ceiling—all became surreal. The blows passed into his body, sending a numbing wave into his groin, on into the mattress, pushing him deep into the springs. At the thirty-sixth stroke, the boy lost track of numbers. Then, without apparent reason, after ten or twelve more, it ended.

For the first time since the beginning, the director spoke: "All right now, get up." The boy tried, but nothing moved. "I said, get on up." The boy again tried to move his legs, to turn, but nothing worked. "If you don't get up off that cot like I told you, we're going to start all over again. Now get up."

Pulling against the bed frame, Mike moved his body from the cot. Pushing, he turned toward the director, who was already looking out the door to the Colored Boys' Room, where Woody was waiting; the long strap hung hot and ready in his hand. An image of a hard-hewn woodcutter awaiting the next load of logs filled the boy's mind. Crying, he finally managed to sit upright on the sagging cot, as Dennis reentered the room.

"All right, boy, stand up, drop your shorts, bend over, and let's have a look at you." Mike finally struggled to his feet as Dennis moved closer. He turned his back to the state men, pulled slowly at the waistband, and drew the shorts to his knees as he bent. "That ain't too bad . . . some bleeding." The director motioned with his hand, talking to Dennis. The boy, head down, looked through his knees. The already mud-smudged, tattered shorts were now blotted with blood.

"OK, you can pull them up. Go with Mr. Dennis and do as he tells you"; the director turned and went into the Colored Boys' Room.

Dennis motioned to Mike to follow him down the corridor. Limping stiff legged, the boy obeyed. "Now you just stand over there in the corner with your face to the wall and wait. Don't make any more noise, or else the director will have you back in that room." It was the first time since entering the White House that Dennis had spoken to the boy. "We'll take you down to the hospital afterward to see to your leg wounds." Dennis left the boy standing face toward the wall, as Woody was taken into the White Boys' Room.

Dennis gone, Mike leaned against the wall, gulping for air, trying to stop the trembling. A few feet to his left, the fan roared on, covering the voices in the White Boys' Room. Suddenly the second round of strokes began, the sound cracking off the walls, echoing into the corridor, breaking in the boy's ears. He slunk to his knees, falling against the wall, covering his eyes with his forearm.

The director again took up his steady rhythm: *Crack-Pow* —two thousand, three thousand, four thousand— *Crack-Pow*. The fifth stroke, the sixth. . . .

The boy pushed his head harder into his arm, but the image of the director swinging the strap over his shoulder and down upon the prone body would not fade. Again and again, he could see it fall.

Between the sixteenth and nineteenth stroke, the boy called Woody began to cry out at each impact. At the twenty-third, the director shouted at him: "Boy, I told you to stuff the corner of that pillow in your mouth and keep it there. I don't want to have to listen to your crying and bawling." The strap fell upon the boy as he got the pillow back into his mouth.

When the twenty-seventh stroke hit Woody, it must have cracked him open. He screamed. A loud, deep, animal cry of agony. Again and again he screamed. As each explosion of leather on ruptured skin broke, he screamed. By the thirty-third, the screaming was one long, continuous wail, rising with each stroke.

After the thirty-sixth stroke, a scuffle broke out in the White Boys' Room. Mike heard the director yell to the other state men, "Get him back on his stomach," and to the boy, "Boy, this is it with you. Now you lay yourself back down there or else we'll send for the kitchen boys. You ain't getting anything you don't deserve. Now lay back down there and take your medicine like a man." Woody was forced back on the cot, and the beating and the wailing began again.

An insane image began to fill Mike's mind. He'd seen it dozens of times at the movies and on the TV: somewhere out West, a fort is surrounded. The last remaining troops of a long seige peer over the stockaded walls. Over a not-too-distant hill, the glow from an Indian camp lights the nocturnal horizon. The cavalry troops are waiting to see if the volunteer sent to get relief makes it through the encircling savages. . . . Suddenly, the silence is broken by a scream. A loud, deep, screaming cry of agony as the volunteer's white skin is ruptured.

Succumbing to hysteria, Mike's scream mixed with those of the boy on the cot.

Finally, the beating stopped. The three state men came out of the White Boys' Room. "What is the matter with you, boy? . . . Do you want some more of the same?" Mike looked up and saw the three pallid-skinned Christians; the tall angular one swinging the blood-wet weapon in his hand. With all his force, with all the resourcefulness he could call upon, he shouted, "I'm praying to Jesus for forgiveness!"

After a long pause, the director spoke again, "Well boy, you just do that, but you'd better do your praying a lot quieter—or else you'll have a lot more to pray about. Now keep quiet, hear me!" Without waiting, he led the state men back into the room, and the beating continued; through forty, forty-five, fifty. At the fifty-sixth stroke, Mike lost count.

He slowly pulled himself to his feet as the sound of the exploding crack of The Paddle and Woody's cries merged into the receding roar of the fan. The pain from the wounds on his foot and leg, from the swollen, cracked flesh of his back and buttocks, melted into rage. It no longer mattered how long, how many blows, or what manner of retribution the state men inflicted. They had done all that was necessary.

SEVENTEEN

Ending Foster-Care Drift

LANIER RAND HOLT
AND JENNIFER MILLER

IN NORTH CAROLINA, A handful of influential citizens and public officials have successfully completed the ponderous process of changing state laws and capturing funds to aid a minority population—children in crisis, children without homes. Thousands of children are tangled in the web of the foster-care system. Before advocates documented their dilemma and moved to ease their plight, children dangled there in unknown numbers and circumstances, powerless to help themselves because they were isolated, poor, had few legal rights, and could not vote. These conditions still hold true, but there is a new impetus toward freeing children from the system.

At its best, a foster-care system provides temporary homes or institutional shelter for children who, for a variety of reasons, cannot stay with their biological parents. At its worst—and as national exposés have revealed of late—the system removes more children than is necessary and then loses sight of its original goals: to aid the natural family and return the child home, or to terminate parents' legal rights in hopeless situations and free the child for adoption. Recent national attention focused on the foster-care system has exposed shockingly large numbers of children taken into state custody and then lost for years in what is commonly called "foster-care drift."

The extent of the problem is

yet unknown because of poor record keeping in the foster-care bureaucracy. Recent estimates are that between 500,000 and 750,000 children nationwide exist in some sort of foster-care arrangement. Over half of these children remain in state custody more than two years and are moved from their foster families or institutions once or twice during their stay in the system; almost 20 percent are moved more than twice, according to the Children's Defense Fund, a private nonprofit child advocacy organization in Washington, D.C. In 1979, the Children's Bureau of HEW reported that 100,000 kids had been in the system *at least six years.* Obviously, for a significant number of children, foster care is not a temporary solution at all.

Seventy years ago, President Teddy Roosevelt stated publicly that children should not be removed from their homes for reasons of poverty alone. Yet poverty and its accompanying characteristics—lack of education, joblessness, inadequate mental care, deficient housing, and lack of resources to prevent and cope with family breakdown—have continuously supplied the foster-care system with its wards. The increase in foster care this century has been proportionately larger than the overall population growth, because poverty has been exacerbated by fragmentation of traditional community and kinship ties in a mobile and industrial nation.

When children are shuttled from one set of strangers to another foster-family home, when every home or institution is temporary for year after crucial year of childhood, irrevocable emotional damage occurs—so says common sense. Research about the long-term effects of foster care is controversial and inconclusive. But public realizations of the possible emotional damage and the certain pain that children in foster care suffer, together with considerations of the long-term costs to the state as these children grow up, often requiring continued welfare services or even incarceration, and the burgeoning expenses of the foster-care system itself all have triggered a unique coalescing of private and public interests for reform.

In North Carolina, as nationally, some social service agencies are welcoming, even eliciting, the aid of leading citizens and child-advocacy organizations in a mutual attempt to gain the support of the highest policymakers and lawmakers for what must be termed an establishment-approved reform plan. The name of this reform is permanency planning. Permanency planning attempts to eliminate one of the worst aspects of the existing system: the long "drift" of children through foster families and institutions. In June 1980, Congress approved, and President Carter signed, a bill which will institutionalize permanency planning nationally if the requested money is in fact appropriated.

Now, at all levels in the foster-care system, the rhetoric is that in most cases biological parents can supply the best homes for their children. Where this is not the case, permanency planners stress that the parents' rights should be legally sundered, freeing the child for adoption. If neither of the first two options is possible, then social service agencies are expected to locate a long-term foster home for the child.

Integral to the permanency planning method is a mandatory public review of each child's case, both in the courtroom and within the social service agency, to ensure that there is a permanent placement plan for the child and that efforts are under way to institute the plan. In localities and states where permanency planning has recently been incorporated into the foster-care system, citizen volunteers are sometimes being drawn into a review process. The volunteer's role is to act as an advocate for the "best interests" of the child and to serve as a buffer between the sometimes antagonistic forces of judicial process and foster-care services. Jan Brukman describes the meeting between caseworker and judge as "the flashpoint of the system, the point where two professional competencies and often two generations of values and morals—can come into conflict." Caseworkers and judges may accuse each other of being either too ready to terminate parental rights or not ready enough. Brukman adds, "Coordinating these professionals is a gargantuan managerial problem, only one of the many reasons permanency planning for foster care is just now officially getting under way in North Carolina."

Permanency planning also strongly favors the court

appointment of a lawyer to represent the child and urges
the rewriting of juvenile legal codes to define more clearly
the rights of biological parents as well as the grounds for
terminating those rights. Definitions of "neglect," "abuse,"
and "dependency"—primary causes for removing children
from their homes—are disturbingly vague and thus open to
interpretation by the various professionals and citizen
volunteers involved in a child's case. In North Carolina, for
example, state law defines a neglected child as one who
does not receive "proper care, supervision or discipline . . .
or who has been abandoned; or who is not provided
necessary medical care or other remedial care recognized
under state law; or who lives in an environment injurious to
his welfare."

In most cases, the individuals who influence the outcome
of children's custody cases—social workers, lawyers,
psychologists, judges, foster parents, and citizen volunteers
—are far removed from the poverty that causes "neglect,"
"abuse," and "dependency." Traditionally, the people
involved in deciding custody cases have been inherently
suspicious of poor people and unimpressed by the strong
bonds which exist, despite hardships, between children and
their natural parents. In *Children in Foster Care,* Gruber
quotes the findings of the State Charities Aid Association of
New York which, in 1960, studied the original home
situations of 100 children in foster care and decided that
over three-fourths of the families "had such a serious
degree of social and economic incompetence as to render
them in all probability beyond the hope of salvage for the
particular child."

Value judgments, motivated by upper-class charitable
mentalities, have contributed in numerous cases to children
being removed from their homes and then never allowed
the chance to return. The national permanency planning
philosophy has turned many heads in the direction of the
biological families, to examine more closely the possibilities
of reunification, to save costs to the state, and to allow
children at least a chance of growing up in a caring family.
The new reform plan does not directly emphasize the need
to increase services and support payments to poor families.
This aid is left to the discretion of advocates and officials

within each state, and in most states remains in the realm of theory, not reality.

In North Carolina, the new reform movement has concentrated on creating a new permanency planning structure atop the old bureaucracy. Reforms of the system were unquestionably necessary to protect children from the impacts of bureaucratic indifference and lack of resources. But permanency planning has little effect on the original families whose children still pack social workers' caseloads and court dockets.

Still, bringing permanency planning to a state traditionally resistant to supporting social services has required a great deal of creative action, coalition building, and personal commitment.

THE MODEL PROGRAM PERMANENCY PLANNING ADVOCATES in North Carolina and other states used for their reform efforts began in Oregon in 1973 in an HEW-funded demonstration project called "Freeing Children for Permanent Placement." Through aggressive planning, casework techniques, and legal action, 90 percent of 520 "hard-to-place" children selected for the project were removed from the temporary foster-care system: 27 percent returned to their natural parents, 52 percent had parental rights terminated and secured adoptive homes, and 11 percent were placed with relatives or with a long-term foster family.

To spread the word about its success, the Children's Bureau funded an outreach program from Oregon to other interested states, providing the uninitiated with staff training, technical assistance, and how-to literature for implementing permanency planning.

Sylvia Stikeleather, director of Foster Care Services within North Carolina's Division of Social Services, and Pat Gustaveson of Group Child Care Consultants, which is affiliated with the University of North Carolina School of Social Work, were determined to bring the Oregon achievements into North Carolina. The Division of Social Services invited staff from the Oregon outreach program to conduct workshops, meetings, and seminars across the state, involving social workers, judges, foster parents, and concerned citizens. Child advocacy organizations in the state were eager to hear about any reform plan. But most North Carolina legislators and top-level administrators were yet unaware of the need for reform.

Clearly, child advocates in the state urgently needed to document the extent of the damage being done to children in the foster-care system. In early 1978, the Governor's Advocacy Council for Children and Youth undertook the project of compiling facts and figures about foster care in the state. In December 1978, the Council published "Why Can't I Have a Home?" and lifted the veils of misinformation and confusion which had shrouded North Carolina's foster-care system from public review. John Niblock says, "The questions we asked weren't complex, but the answers were elusive." The report revealed conditions prevailing in the state to match those coming to light nationally: at least 10,000 children were known to be in the state's foster-care system. Of these, 8,000 were in foster families at the time of the study, while 2,000 were held in child-care institutions or group homes.

The average child in the system has already spent 40 percent of his or her life in foster care, without a permanent home. Significantly, the proportion of children remaining in foster care five years or more increased from 5.4 percent in 1973 to 17.4 percent in 1978. Fewer than 10 percent of these children are orphans.

The natural parents of North Carolina's foster children average $3,150 in yearly income, eight years of schooling, and 50 percent unemployment. The majority are divorced or single. "Child abuse" and "neglect" are the major reasons children are placed in state care. The other major cause is "dependency," which means that the family is unable (because of poverty, perhaps, or alcoholism or a number of other causes) or unwilling to support the child.

Once a child has been removed from its biological family, the majority of parents lose contact with their offspring. Yet natural parents interviewed for the study strongly contended that if social workers had intervened or offered services earlier, the children could have stayed at home. Likewise, half of the judges who responded to the

Council's questionnaire believed that foster-care placement could be prevented by parental training and counseling services. In numerous cases, lack of family financial resources was the sole reason for removing the child.

More factors are at work in the state to encourage removal of children from their natural families than to prevent it. In 1978, the Council found that Aid to Families with Dependent Children (AFDC) payments reached at best only 21 percent of the families in need. Medical care and mental health treatment were provided to only 15 percent and 11 percent, respectively. Services to families with child-raising problems were rare: only 7 percent of the natural parents interviewed had received parental counseling; 5 percent were provided with child-abuse counseling; and only 3 percent had the advantage of day care.

When asked what services would have enabled them to keep their children, the natural parents spoke most often of financial assistance through AFDC, food stamps, job placement, housing assistance, and financial counseling.

North Carolina pays natural parents less in AFDC support to keep their children than it does foster parents for those same children. Overall, the study revealed a state-level willingness to pay 150 percent more to keep a child outside his or her original family. And the average cost of holding a child in one of the state's foster-care institutions is $6,161 a year—almost twice the average yearly income of natural families and twice the average yearly cost of maintaining a child in a foster family.

Foster parents subsidize the state by paying $10 million out of their own pockets for the care of foster children. Also, foster parents receive the same amount in board payments for an adolescent child as they receive for a younger child; they must spend about $1,100 more a year for a sixteen-year-old than for a one-year-old.

The average child stays in foster care twice as long as the average foster-care worker stays on the job, making individual and consistent attention to a child's case nearly impossible. Most caseworkers are overburdened, undertrained, and underpaid, reports the Council. Because of excessively high caseloads—up to eighty cases a worker

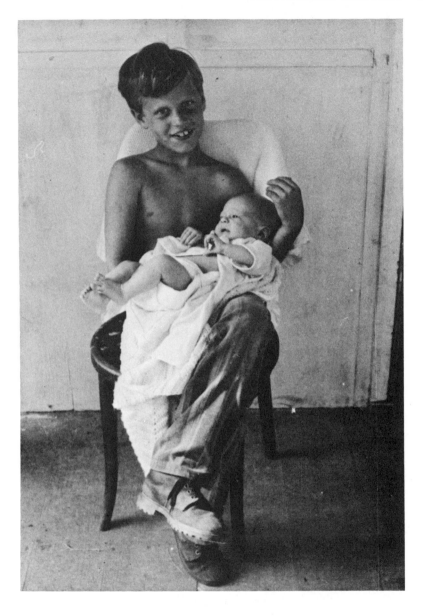

in some North Carolina counties, with an average load of
about twenty-five—combined with administrative duties
and paperwork, caseworkers spend only 12 percent of their
time—an average of forty-eight minutes a month per child
—on direct, in-person contact with their foster children. Yet

the social worker often has sole control over the child until a court review of the case is held, which in many cases happens infrequently and sometimes not at all.

Legislation passed in 1977 instructed district court judges to provide legal representation for children in cases of alleged neglect or abuse. The judge could appoint a lawyer for the child, called a guardian *ad litem,* who would serve as an investigative arm of the court, with powers to obtain confidential information from files, natural parents, foster parents, caseworkers, and others involved. The guardian *ad litem* would then advise the court about the best plan for the child. The Council discovered that almost 40 percent of the judges were not appointing guardians *ad litem* in all of their abuse and neglect cases.

Also in 1977, North Carolina passed a law requiring judges to bring a foster child back to court for a thorough review after the first six months and yearly thereafter, to ensure that some kind of long-term placement plan had been formulated. But the Council found that about 60 percent of the state's district court judges were uncertain about how to conduct a case review or who should schedule it—social services or the court. Judges who did conduct court reviews did so inconsistently: instead of consulting with all persons involved with a child, judges who responded to the Council's questionnaire indicated they rely most on social workers or the child's file for their custody decisions. Least considered, said the judges, were advice and information from the children and their natural parents.

Of 290 children's progress reports surveyed, the Council found that in almost half the cases the child was removed from one foster home and placed in another with no reason given. For the other half, reasons had little to do with the child's wishes or behavior: almost 80 percent of the children were removed because of the personal needs or changes in the foster family.

In the five-county survey, the average child had been placed in two foster homes in less than four years; about 10 percent had been in five or more homes; three children had already been moved ten times! John Niblock wrote,

Foster-care "drift" . . . leads to the child being shunted from one temporary foster home to another, with the resulting loss of attachment and inability to form healthy emotional relationships. . . . The overall impression is that of paper cutouts of young children, alone and helpless, being driven to and fro at the mercy of vagrant winds.

IN EARLY 1979, SYLVIA STIKELEATHER INITIATED AN eight-county volunteer demonstration project—based on the permanency planning model—out of her Foster-Care office in the Division of Social Services.

To qualify, a local agency had to select one social worker whose caseload could not exceed sixteen children (which, without additional staff, meant reduced services for a number of other children during this time). The counties also had to agree to participate in state training sessions, commit some of their supervisor's time to permanency planning efforts, locate adequate legal assistance, provide support services to the families of the children in the experiment, and step up adoption recruitment efforts.

During the year, she provided consultation and workshops for the eight counties chosen on case planning and utilization of legal assistance to ensure that the court proceedings resulted in a permanent home for the child. The year's results in terms of placements were impressive: of the 350 children in the pilot program, 238 were returned home or placed with relatives; 59 were placed through adoption; 21 were in the legal process preceding adoption; 8 remained in long-term foster care; and 24 had "plans pending" with hopes that some might return home. The project's success was later provided to the state's administration and legislature as evidence that permanency planning was both cost-effective and humane.

It is worth noting, however, that the children in this demonstration project were all under the age of twelve. Teenagers are more difficult to place in permanent homes; half of the children in North Carolina's foster-care system are eleven or older. Obviously, Stikeleather was determined to achieve good results in this project in order to sell permanency planning to the state's policymakers. She defends the project's integrity, saying that the children served were both black and white and that other social workers in the county picked up the children dropped from the caseload of the designated permanency planning worker.

WHILE STIKELEATHER WAS CONDUCTING THE DEMONSTRA-tion project aimed at providing the state with proof of the viability of permanency planning, Group Child Care Consultants (GCCC) of the University of North Carolina School of Social Work received a $100,000 grant from the Children's Bureau of HEW. This grant, from the same agency that funded the Oregon project, was designed to step up the pace of transition in North Carolina from foster-care drift to permanency planning. Specifically, the program's aim was to win friends in high places for the ideals of permanency planning. GCCC hoped to educate key representatives of middle-class organizations already involved in children's issues in the state, as well as church leaders, county officials and directors of local social services departments, judges, legislators, and state bureaucrats.

Among the organizations represented in the GCCC year-long series of conferences were several chapters of the Junior League; an association of foster parents, originally formed to sound a collective voice of frustration within the foster-care system; and Action for Foster Children, a broad-based organization of social workers, judges, child-care professionals, and foster parents.

John Niblock was a member of "The Steering Committee to Develop Leadership for Permanency Planning," as was Sylvia Stikeleather's boss in the Division of Social Services. State Senator Willis Whichard also lent the power of his office to the movement and later cosponsored permanency planning legislation in the North Carolina General Assembly.

The first time Stikeleather submitted her permanency planning budget to Secretary Sarah Morrow of the Department of Human Resources, the cutbacks effected by that higher office amounted to "slaughter," according to one official involved in the process; and when the department passed the revised budget along to the State Budget Office, what was left of permanency planning was picked off the skeleton. Nothing remained of the budget for the General Assembly to even consider, much less approve.

In spring 1979, therefore, Niblock presented the Council's recommendations to the legislators in the form of a special bill and budget request. Both the Council and the GCCC steering committee expected that at least a portion of the permanency planning funds would be appropriated that year. Within the agencies and constituencies involved, the reform came highly recommended. The Council's report and the GCCC program had received much attention, which seemed to indicate that the problems in the foster-care system were widely, and publicly, recognized.

"It seemed that the climate was right," says Pat Gustaveson, the permanency planning consultant from GCCC. "With national attention drawn to the issue, solid information in the literature, a state pilot program that was working, and a great deal of local interest statewide, we hoped to be able to move ahead in 1979."

The reform advocates believed that the biggest obstacle to securing funding in 1979 would be the tax-cut fever which had infected Governor James Hunt, as well as many legislators. So they emphasized, in letters and in the legislative halls, that if permanency planning could reduce the average length of stay in foster care by even 10 percent, the investment would more than pay for itself. The state tracking system alone would reduce the number of children staying in foster care unnecessarily long, said Niblock; the system would cost about $76,500 to install and operate for the biennium and would more than pay for itself in the first year of operation. Also, costs to the state are compounded when the disturbed drifters from the foster-care system end up in more restricted institutions: Niblock reported that more than a fourth of the children in North Carolina's training schools were sent there directly from foster-care placement.

These cost-benefit projections, revealing the advantages to the state of reducing the number of children and length of stay in foster care, were heady concepts in the world of public service expenditures.

An additional reason the advocates were optimistic was that in 1979—the International Year of the Child— Governor Hunt had become increasingly vocal in his commitment to the well-being of children in North Carolina. As chair of the Southern Growth Policies Board that year, he was the figurehead for the board's "New Generation" stance, a broad scenario which, through studies, leadership workshops, and conferences, publicly declared the need for improved education, health, and housing for children in the Southern states. With Hunt at the helm, with constituency and citizen backing, and with support from the Division of Social Services, permanency planners were confident that their budget request would be approved.

But when the governor's proposed 1979–1980 budget emerged from the Legislative Advisory Budget Committee, the total permanency planning special request had been left out. "No one knew exactly why," Gustaveson reflected. "Maybe the governor thought other people would be able to take on that particular battle. Maybe our cause was too new to the legislature."

Disappointed by the setback, the Council and some of the steering committee members resolutely stepped up their efforts in the General Assembly throughout the course of the 1979 session, and secured at least an unusual concession from the legislature: they agreed to consider a permanency planning budget in the 1980 short session.

Other pieces of legislation of interest to the Council and steering committee fared better in the 1979 session than the permanency planning appropriations bill. Foster-care board payments were increased somewhat; added to the juvenile code were mandatory appointment of a guardian *ad litem* in child abuse, neglect, and dependency cases and a provision allowing the appointment of an attorney for indigent parents. And the court review procedure was clarified, specifying that the district court judge must consider what services had been offered to the natural family before taking a child into custody, must obtain a permanent plan for the child, and must take into account information and advice of foster parents and natural parents before deciding custody.

As the GCCC leadership training project drew to a close, the most active members of the steering committee formed the Coalition for Foster Children. Its ranks included some of the members of the steering committee and some new representatives of such state organizations as the League of Women Voters, the Black Child Development Institute of North Carolina, the Smoky Mountain Area Mental Health Center, and the North Carolina Association of Black Social Workers—thus broadening their base of support and, significantly, including a few more black representatives in what had previously been an almost all-white committee of advocates for a system in which half the foster-care children are black. The Coalition began holding news conferences in different parts of the state, inviting local legislators to speak up about permanency planning. Each of their organizations joined in the lobbying efforts in their own communities and at the state level.

Perhaps the Coalition's most inspired strategy was the polite pressure it continually applied to Governor Hunt in the months preceding the 1980 session. Several of its members appeared at each of the governor's six hearings, in different sections of the state, in which he gathered grassroots opinions prior to formulating his policies and goals for the coming year. At one such hearing, says coalition member Betty Rose, Governor Hunt appeared, flanked by the heads of several key departments, including Secretary Morrow of the Department of Human Resources; Rose waited for her chance, then stood and said, "Governor Hunt, if we are really concerned about children, let's not forget about those in foster care." A discussion about permanency planning ensued. The persistent campaigners, aided by increased media exposure, began to achieve their desired effect, to the embarrassment of the "New Generation" governor.

Suddenly, to the surprise of all child advocates in the state, Secretary Morrow "redirected" $750,000 of federal child welfare funds to the cost of implementing permanency planning. She explained that the money was not being robbed from the existing foster-care system. Rather, funds had been held for some years by the State Budget Office to conserve state funds; by freeing that money and using it for the existing foster-care system, federal funds could be redirected into the permanency planning program.

The unexpected emergence of this money from the dusty coffers at the heart of state government was a tribute to the untiring efforts of child advocates. It is also another example of the kinds of bureaucratic and political decisions that frustrate delivery of public services in a system where fiscal knowledge is concentrated close to the governor and far away from county service providers and their clients.

The $750,000 was more than half of what the Council had planned to ask for in the special budget request to the 1980 General Assembly. When the short session began, advocates lobbied strenuously in the legislative halls for the remainder of the funds needed for the permanency planning program. This time the legislators responded, allocating all but $58,000 of the request. "It was something of a miracle," commented Senator Whichard. "I think people are sold on the program."

Also quietly passed in the short session was a controversial bill expanding the circumstances under which parental rights may be terminated. Under this new law, if a natural parent can be proven "mentally incompetent," the offspring will be legally freed for adoption. Safeguards to this procedure, according to Niblock, are that the parent may be represented by a court-appointed attorney and that

the judge is supposed to require testimony from a
psychologist or other professional who will state that the
parent will never recover from his or her incapacity.

Actual implementation of permanency planning will
undoubtedly vary from county to county in North Carolina.
As of this writing, $650,000 of the funds appropriated for
the total program will be divided among the state's 100
counties if they request it. To receive the funds, counties
must submit a plan to Sylvia Stikeleather's foster-care
office in the Division of Social Services, specifying how
they will meet the permanency planning criteria. Briefly,
they are required to use the funds to set up a team of
social workers to review cases regularly; hire a permanency
planning specialist and keep his or her caseload at a
maximum of sixteen children; receive training and
supervision from the state; have access to an attorney
knowledgeable about foster-care issues to aid in the
necessary court processes; provide support services to
natural parents and foster parents; set up an adoption
recruitment service and refer adoptable children that they
cannot place to the state level. And counties are being
urged to concentrate their permanency planning efforts on
children under twelve, for whom placement is most likely
to be successful.

One problem with North Carolina's plan, which the
advocates have decided they can live with, is the
distribution formula. Permanency planning funds will not in
all cases be placed where the need is most extreme. The
Budget and Planning Office of the Department of Human
Resources decided, despite Stikeleather's and Niblock's
initial objections, to divide the $650,000 on the basis of
each county's population rather than on the number of
children in foster care. It is generally true that the most
populous counties have the largest number of children in
foster care. Yet dividing the funds by population means that
appropriations to large counties will be in the tens of
thousands of dollars, while the smallest counties will
receive only a few hundred dollars.

The rest of the funds appropriated for permanency
planning (over $40,000) will be used to set up the state
tracking system, to strengthen the state adoption exchange,

and to hire state-level permanency planning staff and supervisors. Stikeleather plans a head count of children helped by the new system in four to six months and says, "I think the program will show results."

THE COALITION NOW CONTINUES TO WORK ON ONE ASPECT of permanency planning which must be incorporated county by county. Called the Children in Placement Program (CIP), it is a postplacement monitoring process for use by district court judges hearing placement cases of children removed from their homes because of alleged neglect, abuse, or dependency. Already, the recent changes in North Carolina law require judges to periodically review the child's case and to appoint a guardian *ad litem* to represent the child's best interest. Additionally, the CIP program has as its objective the inclusion of more citizen volunteers as monitors, to ensure that court reviews are indeed scheduled, to review case files, to talk to children, their natural parents, their foster parents, and their social workers, and to act as the child's advocate in the courtroom. CIP projects are under way in five of North Carolina's 100 counties.

Members of the Coalition and the Council, and now the CIP volunteers, have several things in common: they share a concern for children caught in the limbo of foster care, and they are devoting time and energy to that cause. They represent or are individually recognized as powers in the state. They are not challenging the bureaucratic system which structurally exhibits a distrust of the poor. Instead they are applying their efforts within it. And they are, by and large, far removed from the poverty and its symptoms which have caused the foster-care system to become what it is today.

Members of the Coalition, especially, are shocked by the situations they have encountered with natural parents who drink heavily, who have no food in the house, or who can't even pay the rent for an apartment; they speak about the child covered with cigarette burns, the mother who lost contact with her child but still would not agree to legally terminate her relationship, about battered and neglected and undisciplined children who simply must be taken care of. One woman said, as if surprised, "Most abused children have an attachment to their parents. You let the child, he'll go back to the parents that abused him."

Of course, they are equally horrified by stories of children "lost" in the foster-care system. Another member of the Coalition told the story of an infant freed for adoption who nevertheless spent eighteen years in various foster homes; another child was forgotten for years until his case file was discovered behind an office cabinet. And they speak about the heartbreak of children arbitrarily removed from foster parents whom they love.

When asked if the Coalition's long and vigorous reform campaign had perhaps skirted the problem of poverty for the majority of natural parents of foster children, one member responded: "I want AFDC payments to be higher, but when you are up to your armpits in alligators, it's hard to concentrate on draining the swamp."

Interestingly, this same analogy appears, almost word for word, in a report from the Oregon project prepared for the Children's Bureau of HEW. But in the Oregon project report, the alligator analogy is followed by a qualifier: "Nonetheless, what we really have to do is drain the swamp. We do have to get kids out of care and into permanent homes. But we also have to prevent children from entering care inappropriately in the first place."

Time will tell on permanency planning in North Carolina. It will likely reduce the number of children who drift for years through the foster-care system. But will many of these children be returned, without the resources they need, to the same desperate home situations which originally motivated Social Services and the courts to take them into state custody? Plagued by these questions and others, Duke University anthropologist Jan Brukman is less than jubilant about the motivations for permanency planning and its potential results in North Carolina.

These people convinced legislators with figures about how the cost of the foster-care system will be reduced over the years with permanency planning. But permanency planning will be effective to the degree of resources put into it—more people and more money, more children will be placed. It's like the Great Society programs of the '60s—they proved to be expensive beyond anybody's reckoning. People just don't have the data to predict whether permanency planning will cut costs. But that should be irrelevant. Children have to have homes.

SOURCES

Fanshel, David, and Shinn, Eugene B. *Children in Foster Care: A Longitudinal Investigation.* New York: Columbia University Press, 1978.

Gruber, Alan R. *Children in Foster Care.* New York: Human Sciences Press, 1978.

Jeter, Helen R. *Children, Problems and Services in Child Welfare Programs.* In cooperation with Child Welfare League of America, U.S. Department of HEW, Welfare Administration, Children's Bureau. Washington, D.C.: U.S. Government Printing Office, 1963.

Knitzer, Jane; Allen, Mary Lee; and McGowan, Brenda. *Children Without Homes.* Washington, D.C.: Children's Defense Fund, 1978.

Maas, Henry S., and Engler, Richard E., Jr. *Children in Need of Parents.* New York: Columbia University Press, 1959.

North Carolina Department of Administration. *Why Can't I Have a Home? Foster Care and Adoption in North Carolina.* Raleigh, North Carolina: Governor's Advocacy Council on Children and Youth, 1978.

EIGHTEEN

Words Suffused Our Lives

ALLAN TROXLER

FIRST TO MOURN THE passing of old libraries. The massive front doors that opened with a struggle; the dim vestibules; the gleaming linoleum on squeaky floors; the worn, hollow-sounding stairs that climbed up into the thin, hot air of balconies and down to gloomy basements where my bare feet walked cautiously on the cool, sweaty cement. How delicious, on summer afternoons, to have wandered off into a book and still to listen to the thunder roll away across town, the rain splash from the eaves, cars hiss past, and the doors to the children's room swing idly, *thuhdump thuhdump.* There was such satisfaction in watching the librarian's pencil flip back and forth from the writing end to the eraser, where she had stuck that little stamp, and just like that, in purple ink by the name, was "Aug. 14, 1955."

The old library had been a church, and then a hospital for Confederate soldiers. Through the doors on the far side of the children's room, up a curving sweep of stairs that made me lightheaded, was the Historical Museum, where Martha Arnold's grandfather's artifacts from the Holy Lands reposed in dusty glass cases alongside ancient Miss Nina Troy's dolls from China, where she had been a Methodist missionary. There was a petrified cat someone had found under their front porch, and a knit hat with a black splotch which, the sign said,

151

was the blood of a Revolutionary War soldier. So you could read until your bottom ached, and then wander up to the museum or out to the derelict cemetery behind the building, and then return to the children's room to read some more. Then they moved all the books and the librarian to a huge glass-and-concrete box a few blocks away, about the time I entered junior high school, and the spell was broken.

"I have raised my children to do better and to be better than I am," said my great-grandfather in a history of Haywood County, North Carolina. Prevented from farming by a Civil War bullet that left him lame, he was a great reader, recited Milton and Shakespeare, and was the first in the valley to send his daughters, as well as his sons, off to college. Books were the agent of each generation's improvement. Mother remembers sitting in an apple tree, at age nine, reading Dickens. At the time, books expressly for children were rare; for many, the Bible was the only book in the house, and it was a rich and confusing source of myth and image. In first grade, Mrs. Griffin led us through the Twenty-Third Psalm every morning: "Surely goodness and mercy will follow me all the days of my life." To this day, the Valley of the Shadow of Death and the cup that runneth over are imbued with six-year-old mystery for me. An aunt wrote children's stories drawn from the exploits of her nieces and nephews, so we read about ourselves in *Wee Wisdom* and *Humpty Dumpty.* Our own poems and stories were mimeographed in the elementary school magazine, and our theatricals gave life to the fairy tale of the hour. The practice of words suffused our lives.

The child and the adult speak to each other in the Southern storytelling tradition and often the voices become one. Many Southern novels and short stories are told with children's voices. And certainly adults take their storytelling for children very seriously. From tales lovingly told long ago to recent books that contribute to the unfolding of a regional sense of self, the children's literature of the South is broad and deep.

What follows is a chronological list of books for children by Southern writers and about the South. The selection is purely idiosyncratic, drawn from old favorites and recent discoveries.

Elsie Dinsmore, by Martha Finley, 1868.

What a dreadful, exquisitely unpleasant book. Elsie cries, or
rather weeps, for joy, remorse, or religious ecstasy on most
of 316 pages. The book is emphatically racist, classist, and
ageist—the central conflict is between little Elsie's piety and
her father's insistence that he, not Jesus, is the final word.
So why is this book on my list? It is instructive. Ms. Finley's
didactic intentions backfire, and we learn a different lesson
altogether. What is wrong with *Elsie Dinsmore* is its
complete disregard for the complexity of human affairs.
Elsie is flat as a pancake, the other characters are either
good or bad, and her father is Episcopalian.

   This simplification is a temptation to which many
contemporary writers for children, of all persuasions,
succumb. They labor to conceal their preachments in
implausible situations, or, point-blank, make literal plays for
little minds. I can't imagine children benefiting from such
stuff. If you find *Elsie Dinsmore* hard to put down, as have
thousands of neurasthenic tykes, I recommend Saki's tale,
"The Story Teller," as a corrective. All through *Elsie
Dinsmore* I thought of Bertha, whose clinking medals for
Goodness give her away to a ravening wolf.

The Conjure Woman, by Charles Waddell Chesnutt,
1899.

The important role of voice in *The Conjure Woman* must
derive from the dichotomies of Chesnutt's life: born a free
black, in 1866 he moved to North Carolina at age eight
and there experienced the virtual serfdom that prevailed for
ex-slaves; in 1883, he returned to Ohio to become a
lawyer, when that profession was even more exclusively
white than it is today; he knew both South and North
intimately. The "I" of the book is a smug young white
planter, and right off Chesnutt seems to be laughing, or at
least smiling, at the narrator's confidence in white science.

   On the first trip to their future plantation, narrator and
wife meet "a venerable-looking colored man" sitting on a
log and going at a hatful of scuppernongs. Uncle Julius.
Immediately, Chesnutt limns the uneasy space the two men
are to inhabit through the book:

*"Is you de Norv'n gemman w'at's gwine ter buy de ole
vimya'd?"*

*"I am looking at it," I replied; "but I don't know that I
shall care to buy unless I can be reasonably sure of
making something out of it."*

*"Well, I dunno whe'r you b'lieves in conj'in' er not,
some er de w'ite folks don't, er says dey don't,—but de
truf er de matter is dat dis yer ole vimya'd is goophered."*

*"Is what?" I asked, not grasping the meaning of this
unfamiliar word.*

"Is goophered,—conju'd, bewitch'."

*He imparted this information with such earnestness,
and with such an air of confidential mystery, that I felt
somewhat interested, while Annie was evidently much
impressed, and drew closer to me.*

"How do you know it's bewitched?"

And so the author uses the dryly logical "I" as setting
and foil for Uncle Julius's dark, powerful conjure tales—an
effective device for exploring the confrontation of white
male rationalism and black spiritualism. With his stories of
"haints," Uncle Julius defends the old, naturalized vineyard,
the forest, and the swamp from the incursions of progress.
In an autocracy where the great majority of people—
women, slaves, poor whites, and children—couldn't speak
their minds, stories were both protection and subversion.

The tales are windows onto slavery, and not a bit rose-
colored. The practice of conjuring among slaves has been
glossed over by historians. Just like the narrator, they
cannot be expected to understand magic. But children will.

Two Little Confederates, by Thomas Nelson Page,
illustrated by John W. Thompson, 1888.

I am torn about this book. The slaves are loyal wily
buffoons, the two white boys are brave little soldiers, and
the white women are beautiful, long-suffering, and proud.
Still, it seems valuable in deep ways I didn't expect when I
began reading it. In this gracefully written story of what
Frank and Willy experience of war, Page takes us on many
adventures: apprehending a chicken thief, trapping a family

of feral hogs, and hunting for deserters. And then, as the boys watch a skirmish swing back and forth and end in a rout for the rebels, the awful confusion and loss and pain of war catch up with them, and us.

Fleeing the bullets that whistle through the trees "with a long, singing 'zooee,' " they come upon a Yankee soldier lying in the woods, calling for water; it is the soldier who had captured the boys earlier that day:

He could not raise his hand now. There was a pause. The boys stood around, looking down on him. "I've come back home," he said. His eyes were closed.

Young Soldiers from "Two Little Confederates"

"He's dreaming," whispered Willy.
"Did you ever see anybody die?" asked Frank, in a low tone.
Willy's face paled.

The soldier imagines that he is back in Delaware with his boy at bedtime, and Frank and Willy recite their prayers with him, and then:

The boys waited, but that was all. The dusk settled down in the woods. The prayer was ended.
"He's dead," said Frank, in deep awe.
"Frank, aren't you mighty sorry?" asked Willy in a trembling voice. Then he suddenly broke out crying.
"I don't want him to die! I don't want him to die!"

Grandfather Tales, by Richard Chase, illustrated by Berkeley Williams, Jr., 1948.

There is no book like *Grandfather Tales.* Chase takes an abundance of stories, customs, songs, nonsense, and even a play and wraps them up cleverly in the recreation of a mountain family's Old Christmas Eve. This book is a marvel of "appropriate scholarship." I can't imagine a better use for Chase's exhaustive research and knowledge of folk culture. How fortunate he didn't throw it all into the maw of Academe, fattening on unread dissertations. Each of Chase's stories is in itself wondrous, and he trusts the ancient, simple powers of the voice to charm the listener.

If you're looking for adventure, here's "The Outlaw Boy," a Robin Hood account that came down the centuries by word of mouth. If you want romance, here are "Catskin" and "Whitebear Whittington," first cousins to "Cinderella" and "Beauty and the Beast." For macabre, manic humor, there's "Old Dry Frye," and "The Skoonkin Huntin" for ebullient nonsense. "Like Meat Loves Salt," collected from a seventh grade girl in Wise, Virginia, is a touching retelling of the King Lear story.

Oh, the tales go on and on, through the long night around the fire in the little cabin. At last the door is opened, and everybody files out into the cold, early light

The Mummer's Play in *Grandfather Tales*

and the newfallen snow. Then the old folks who are left get
out a tattered *Southern Harmony* and sing ''The Babe of
Bethlehem,'' and you can hear every quavering note.

THERE'S A STACK OF BOOKS ON MY TABLE THAT I HAVEN'T
told you about yet. Maybe you're familiar with them, so I'll
just mention a few. *The Bat Poet* is Randall Jarrell's limpid

and wistful allegory of the lonely artist, who still finds his/her snug place when winter sets in. There's no question that the misunderstood bat was, in part, Jarrell. *The Bat Poet* is peerless bedtime reading-aloud material.

When I was little, there were no books in our old library like *Roll of Thunder, Hear My Cry,* by Mildred Taylor, or *Ludell,* by Brenda Wilkinson. These idiomatic stories of black girls growing up in Mississippi and Georgia are, for the white reader, shocking, long overdue summonses to understanding.

In the scramble to purvey liberated, nonsexist stories to children, the listmakers always overlook the cleverest saboteurs of all—Louise Fitzhugh and James Marshall. Although Fitzhugh was Southern, she spent her writing life in New York and wrote about the city, so I can refer you to *Harriet the Spy* and *Nobody's Family Ever Changes* only as an aside. James Marshall was born in Texas, and that's the setting for *Bonzini! The Tattooed Man.* To my way of thinking, it's much more to the point than all the books about boys who knit combined.

The wind blew harder, the wagon rolled faster, and A.W., afraid Bonzini might never return, ran after him.
"Bonzini! Wait for me! Please take me with you!"
But the wind howled, and Bonzini yelled back, "I can't wait! I can't stop the wind!"

But he comes back in the end.

NINETEEN

Afrikan-Americans Educate Their Own

WEKESA MADZIMOYO

FEW AFRIKAN-AMERICAN women have enjoyed the luxury of staying at home to raise the children on a full-time basis. Many more have instead sought affordable child-care arrangements to enable them to extend their education or enroll in job training programs, as well as to work.

But as more parents go into the job market, as the rate of teenage pregnancies increases, and as a greater number of single parents find themselves the lone providers for their children, the waiting lists for day-care centers grow longer. Meanwhile, the cost of quality day care spirals upward. Given the staggering unemployment rate among Afrikan-Americans (14.2 percent overall and 36 percent for Afrikan-American youth) and the widening earned-income gap between whites and Afrikan-Americans, day-care cost increases are particularly devastating for Afrikan-Americans.

The fact that most day-care centers do not meet the particular needs of Afrikan-American children and families presents as great a problem as that of finding day care at all. Federal policies exacerbate the problem by placing limited emphasis on parent input or on training parents to work in the centers. Many government officials and day-care providers proclaim their commitment to preschool education related to the child's family, community, and culture. Yet Afrikan-American families most often encounter programs whose treatment and misunderstanding of their culture and aspirations do Afrikan-American children a grave disservice.

Most day-care programs are based on theories and models developed largely by white educators and psychologists. All too often, standardized IQ and language examinations still form part of early childhood assessment, even though many of these tests have been proven inaccurate and culturally biased. More importantly, these methods have lowered teachers' motivation and their expectations for Afrikan-American youth.

A recent Health, Education and Welfare (HEW) publication, entitled "The Lasting Effects after Pre-School," states: "Head Start programs were initiated in the hope that changing children's attitudes and abilities would be instrumental in extracting them from poverty." In other words, this multimillion-dollar program was based upon the premise that Afrikan-Americans are themselves the primary cause of their own poverty. This is a classic case of "blaming the victim" and is just one of the assumptions held by the dominant society which directly or indirectly affect day-care programming. Other such assumptions relate to Afrikan-American language (that it is simply broken English), family structure (that it is characterized by broken homes or illegitimate children), child-rearing practices (that they are too harsh), concern about community improvement (that it is lacking), and the ability to make constructive decisions about their own condition (that it doesn't exist). Much too often these are reflected in the centers' teaching methodology, organizational structure, and curriculum or program design. Too few centers are organized to include parents as program planners and decision makers.

Analogous to the agonizing forced separation of family members inflicted upon Afrikan-Americans during the chattel slavery experience is the separation (alienation) which this society and its educational institutions, including day-care centers, require low-income Afrikan-American parents to endure. Think of it—low-income Afrikan-American children are taught that (and required to act as if) the values, language, behaviors, and fears of their parents and relatives are wrong. Their community is directly or indirectly depicted as a malignant cancer (called the ghetto, the slums, the projects, etc.) from which escape is a must. In most curricula, Afrikan and Afrikan-American history and culture are excluded. The use of European-American texts and materials forces Afrikan children to experience heroism, intrigue, humor, and fantasy through the eyes and words of white Americans. And most centers teach nothing of what it means to be of Afrikan descent in this racist society.

For example, many Afrikan-American parents follow a West Afrikan tradition of deleting the "th" sound and replacing it with a "d" (as in "dis" for "this") or "f" (as in "Souf" instead of "South"). They usually continue to use these Afrikan-American linguistic substitutions even after their children have eagerly shared their most recent English lesson—"Mama, my teacher said that we supposed to say '*th*at,' not '*d*at.' " The result is alienation. The children are made to feel ashamed of their parents' language. The parents, although joyful that their children are receiving a "good education," feel helpless and angry as they become subtly isolated from their own children. Parents hear the society's negative views of them, their communities, their Afrikan race and culture uttered innocently through the lips of their own children. The accompanying pain makes poignantly clear the failure of the educational programs in most traditional centers, as it emphasizes the historically oppressed condition endured by Afrikan-Americans in this country.

In the teaching of language, how much more wholesome it would be to teach Afrikan-American children their community's expression of their Afrikan culture—including linguistic responses to the English language and oppression —as well as standard English as a second (but not optional) language. Children could then learn to use the language appropriate to a particular setting rather than being forced unwittingly to promote European cultural dominance. How much more affirmative of the family and motivating to the child it would be to solicit from parents family customs, folk tales, songs, and history and to incorporate this heritage into the formal lesson plans. To do less is to drive a wedge between children and their pasts and to divide them from significant portions of themselves.

Many Afrikan-Americans believe, further, that education suitable for Afrikan-Americans depends less on equal access to any kind of preschooling or public education offered and more on the character and quality of the education received. Asa Hilliard III, dean of the School of Education at San Francisco State University, has compared the instruction currently provided by traditional early childhood educational centers with the training of sheep dogs. In an

Ahidiana Work/Study Center in New Orleans

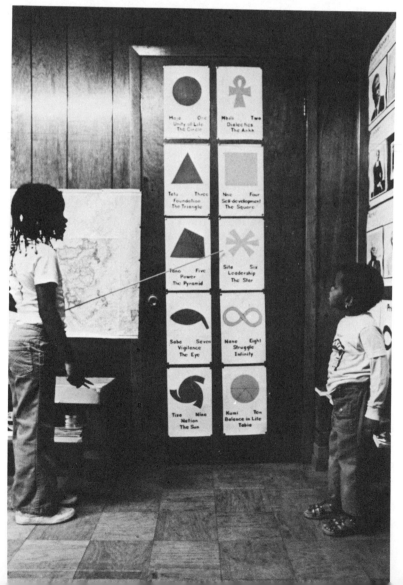

article published in the *Black Child Advocate* entitled *"In Loco Parentis* or Retrieving Responsibility," he concludes that Afrikan-Americans have accepted "training" for education and as a result often become "living, breathing, highly skilled, quite intelligent robots. . . . As black people in America at this very moment we continue to pay a terrible price for what is happening to the minds of our children."

Afrikan-Americans have traditionally challenged the education prescribed by the dominant society. The increasing expressions of outrage and the forming of alternatives for Afrikan-American education represents a revival of a similar movement which reached its apex in the early nineteenth century. In 1838, Afrikan-American activist M.H. Freeman prefigured today's discussion of the effect of oppression on self-concept: "Our oppressed condition in this country has rendered us deficient in the first essential of true manhood—self-respect. Thus in early childhood the circumstances that surround [the Afrikan-American youth's] parents and the treatment received from the community all tend to diminish his respect and reverence for them, hence to deprecate his respect for himself."

While Freeman drew connections between formal and informal education and oppression, one of the revolutionary giants of that period, David Walker, specifically criticized the superficial instruction that white teachers and schools provided Afrikan children. In his *Appeals to the Coloured Citizens of the World* (1829), he illuminated the fact that the goal of white educators was to create in Afrikan-Americans a servile mentality and behavior. Walker advocated that Afrikan-Americans should educate themselves: "Remember to let your aims, your labour, among your brethren and particularly the youth, be the dissemination of education." Acknowledging the self-hatred prevalent among Afrikan-Americans, he advised this cure:

Never mind what the ignorant ones among us say, many of who when we speak to them for their own good, and try to enlighten their minds, laugh at you, and perhaps

*tell you plump to your face, that they want no instruction
from you or any other Niger and all such aggravating
language. Now if you are a man of understanding and
sound sense, I conjure you . . . to impute their actions to
ignorance, and wink at their follies, and do your best to
get around them some way or other, for they are your
brethren; and I declare to you that it is for your own
interest to teach and enlighten them.*

Walker proclaimed that the goal of Afrikan-American
education should be to achieve freedom from oppression
by any means necessary and to establish an independent
nation of Afrikan peoples. In the same spirit, free Afrikans,
opposing the quality of education their children were
receiving in Boston's integrated public schools, removed
their children in the 1820s and established schools in local
Afrikan-American churches.

THE REVIVAL OF THIS CRITICAL AND INDEPENDENT THRUST
during the last fifteen years has resulted in new definitions
of educational goals and basic skills for Afrikan-American
youth. A curriculum minimally suited for Afrikan-American
children of any age should include much more than the
traditional cognitive skills; it should direct the children
toward answering questions relevant to their lives as
Afrikan-Americans and to their goal of liberation from
racial, economic, and cultural oppression: questions like
where did we come from; what is happening to us; who
are we; how can our condition be changed; what is my
goal; and who am I.

Afrikan-American community leaders, educators, and
parents are advocating community control of existing
day-care centers and schools. They are also establishing
independent schools to educate their children about their
own history, present struggle, and future aspirations.

The Federation of Child-Care Centers of Alabama
(FOCAL) advocates community control of educational
resources in Alabama. FOCAL encourages independent
planning at local levels and provides both technical and
resource assistance. Through FOCAL, Afrikan-American

community groups are forging educational goals and programs appropriate to their children and establishing standards which guide both teachers and parents. Organized in 1972, FOCAL exists today as a statewide federation of community-controlled day-care center operators and advocates. Through the *Federation Update* (its bimonthly publication), FOCAL's 650-plus members keep abreast of national and state child-care legislation, child nutrition, CETA programming, new or continuing issues in early childhood education, and program development. FOCAL members serve in policymaking groups, testify before national and state legislators, and speak before groups and organizations concerned with children.

Six months after FOCAL was organized, a conference was held in Frogmore, South Carolina, to develop a national black educational system. The emerging group of twenty-eight people, representing fourteen independent schools across the nation, committed themselves to organizing "the many independent educational institutions presently in operation into a uniform pattern of educational achievement, devoted to correct political objectives and dedicated to excellence." Toward this end, they formed the Council of Independent Black Institutions (CIBI).

Like FOCAL, CIBI provides resources and technical assistance at little or no cost to community groups interested in Afrikan-American education. CIBI maintains a Teacher Training Institute and an Afrikan Teacher Corps. The Teacher Training Institute is designed to develop "dedication, discipline, and dependability" among teachers while also outlining correct ideology, curriculum content, and teaching methods. The Afrikan Teacher Corps consists of institute graduates who agree to serve CIBI for one year in an assigned location. According to CIBI, "Our schools are training and educating our children to become revolutionaries, leaders and workers for our people."

CIBI's member schools and other independent black schools advocate and practice financial as well as ideological independence. The hardships this philosophy engenders are real and are amplified in these times of inflation and unemployment. However, a significant number of Afrikan-American parents feel (as did their forebears in nineteenth-century Boston) that the freedom and the educational results merit the sacrifice. Most independent Afrikan Free Schools are located in the North and West, but several exist in major Southern cities. These include the Learning House in Atlanta, the Black and Proud School in Jackson, Mississippi, and the Ahidiana Work/Study Center in New Orleans.

Although no two schools are exactly alike, they all oppose traditional Western approaches to education, which have created a gulf between ideology and technology or academics. "We are convinced," asserts Ahidiana's Kalamu Salaam, "that it does make a difference whether the computer programmer is political or apolitical. Therefore, our goal is to develop technical competence and academic excellence among politicized people."

Atlanta's Learning House, now a decade old, seeks to politicize its children by teaching them about the true nature of America and the true needs of Afrikan people. The center has initiated new rituals appropriate to Afrikan-American struggles. For example, at birthday celebrations, the "honored" children help prepare the vegetarian meal for the celebration. They present something they have learned or created during the past year and make a pledge for something they wish to accomplish in the coming year.

At Ahidiana the familiar nursery rhymes give way to songs designed to help the children think about their identity: "Are we tables? No! Are we backwards? No! Are we Afrikan? *Ye bo* [Kiswahili for yes]! Are we negroes? No! Are we? . . ."

The teachers also shun traditional workbooks, posters, and text materials; instead, they create their own. Ahidiana currently prints and publishes two books: *Who Will Speak For Us?/New Afrika Folk Tales,* and *Herufi: An Alphabet Reader.* The teachers have written a teaching manual and plan to publish it within the next year. Handmade posters teach that *A* is for "Afrika," *B* is for "build," and *C* is for "create." Multicolored flash cards illustrate indigenous Afrikan geometric shapes and what they mean.

All these schools are vegetarian and put great emphasis

Young Student at Ahidiana

on nutrition. The children at the Learning House grow a backyard garden. Parent-teacher Amoye Wa feels that this experience teaches responsibility and inspires confidence and independence in the children. To encourage a similar diet at home, Ahidiana sponsors vegetarian cooking workshops and readily responds to parents who say, "My child says he wants some avocados, but I don't know how to prepare them."

In addition to nutrition workshops, the schools instruct

parents in various aspects of Afrikan-American child care. They are encouraged, and in some cases required, to participate in certain aspects of the school's program. Getting parents to participate is easier in these schools than in many traditional centers, for these parents have already made the conscious decision to take an active hand in their children's education. They often teach on a full-time, part-time, or substitute basis and volunteer to do other work. Without this strong support from parents, the schools would have a hard time maintaining high staff-child ratios and low tuition ($75 a month at Ahidiana, $130 at the House).

Even with this support, staying solvent and sane is quite a task. But parents and teachers believe that Afrikan-American parents who participate in the education of their children will witness a new clarity in their own perception and planning. At Ahidiana they say, "Our struggle to educate our children has led us to assess our history and conditions, develop a rationale and ideology to guide our present course of action, and finally to project a vision of our future development."

DUE TO INCREASED OCCUPATIONAL SPECIALIZATION AND overreliance on so-called experts, parents rarely find or forge the clarity of purpose or direction in evidence at Ahidiana. Too many Afrikan-American parents surrender their responsibility to shape their own lives, plan their own future, and educate their own children. Too often this responsibility falls to "experts" whose values, attitudes, and actions represent only subtler versions of their slaveholding forebears. Even more burdensome for Afrikan-Americans is the loss of know-how and the resulting dependence which accompanies parents' inactivity. However, the tide may be turning; it is becoming increasingly evident that Afrikan-Americans who have long pushed for self-education are being joined by increasing numbers of others. Some of these parents pressed for integration to achieve good education for their children but are now dissatisfied with the results: the decrease in community control of schools and day-care centers, the decline in their children's overall achievement levels, and the racist values stressed in the public school and traditional day-care systems. More and more parents are pondering the relationship between education and oppression. And as more Southern Afrikan-American parents reject capitalism, racism, and sexism as avenues to the good life, the search for and framing of alternative postures of living and learning are bound to increase.

SOURCES

Bell, Derrick. "The Curse of Brown on Black." *First World Magazine,* 2, no. 1 (Spring 1978): 14–18.

Hilliard, Asa G. "'In Loco Parentis' or Retrieving Responsibility." *The Black Child Advocate,* 7, nos. 2 and 3 (May 1979): 5–8.

Brochure from The Council of Independent Black Institutions 1978–1979. P.O. Box 232, Oberlin, Ohio 44074.

Interviews with Kalamu ya Salaam of Ahidiana and Amoye Wa, director of Learning House.

Stuckey, Sterling. "The Spell of Africa." Ph.D. dissertation, Northwestern University, 1973.

TWENTY

My Life with Sports

ALLAN TROXLER

A BOY DANCES IN THE feverish shade under the trees. He glistens as he turns and turns and turns. Beethoven blares from the house. The boy wears baggy shorts with an elastic waistband. It's 1955. He's about to take a long, painful journey from which he's still returning.

Home movie: blue-shadowed children play on glaring sand. Susan prances with seaweed on her head; Becky smiles uneasy smile of youngest; Nancy looks up from sand castle, scowls, speaks; Chris jumps around in surf; I hold up a shell. Angel wing, scallop, conch, baby's ear, coral, cockle.

I wandered many hours on Long Beach those summers, looking, looking. Bags full of shells. In the dark heat, lightning flashed and waves rumbled and hissed. "Shrimp boats are a-comin', their sails are in sight, shrimp boats are a-comin', there's dancin' tonight," I sang bravely as I walked at night on the squeaking sand. Riding waves once, suddenly there was nothing under my feet. Thrashing, screaming, going under. My brother pulled me in.

In Greensboro in the evening suffused with honeysuckle and clematis, we played croquet. When it got too dark to see the balls, we tossed sticks high as we could and watched bats streak across the dim sky. When it got too dark for that, we watched the lightning bugs blink and slowly rise. I lived comfortably in my body then.

Daddy would take us bowling. In the event that I knocked over any pins, a colored man appeared from nowhere and set them back up.

In the woods—the climbing tree, the owl tree, the hideout under the eleagnus below the ballfield, the big hole in the base of a tulip poplar, full of black water that wiggled. Forever, on autumn afternoons, I journeyed from island to island in that sea of sibilant leaves. Now I reach up to touch easily the dogwood branches where I used to climb, fearless and dizzy, and sit until called for supper.

Before play became sports, before my friends and I graduated to the sexual strife of our adolescent elders, there was sling-the-statue and mother-may-I in the backyard, red light and roller bat. I painted and drew and sculpted exuberantly. We went fishing out at Cousin Lizzie's. Richard Taliaferro and I roller-skated to school, to the great chagrin of Mrs. Sears, policelady. "Stop the cars!" we'd holler, careening down Dellwood and past her station at Cornwallis, unable to brake. I dawdled in the locker room at Lindley Park Pool to watch the naked bodies of the older boys and the men. Eventually, they closed the pool to keep the Negroes out.

Then, one summer, I went to Y camp, I thought I'd make friends and do arts and crafts and play in the lake. Instead, I struggled to be promoted from Guppy to Minnow, or Minnow to Guppy, and wasn't. I became afraid of the water. On carnival day, in a sweltering tent, a handsome counselor brandished a jockstrap, which was the punch line to a joke I didn't understand. By the campfire one night, the boy who was It never guessed right and ended stripped of all but the paper bag over his head. Then in the dwindling light, we all sang "The Old Rugged Cross." In the Chapel in the Woods, we learned about the Lake of Fire and the Seven Trumpets. On Parents' Day, I fled to the toilet labeled "His'n" and wept.

A snapshot: I wear a somber dress that hangs limply around my ankles. Navy blue, at best, with tiny dots. Probably from Miss Effie, grandmother, Methodist preacher's wife. Heavy black heels, small black hat with net, menacing pocketbook, serious face. I am seven or eight.

The footlocker filled with mildewed clothes from female relatives was a magic place, just as the backyard ballfield was for my brother. I chugged around in high heels as easily as sneakers. Pants and shirts, and a suit on Sunday, were uniforms. Dress-ups were expression and amplification. But then on the playground at school someone told me I ran like a girl. Douglas Banner peed in the dress-up box, and one afternoon when I saw some friends coming up the driveway, I ran to my room, slammed the door, and tore off my costume.

Home movie, 1956: on the terrace behind the house, boys eat hotdogs. My birthday. Brooks Harrell, Jimmy Morris, Ed Moore, Wesley Graves, others. They would rather play baseball than run relay races, but it's my party and the testing is only about to begin. Somebody gives me a baseball bat.

The summer of 1958, I painted my violin case silver and went to the string institute over at the women's college. Ed,

Wesley, Jimmy, and Brooks went off to sports camp at the coast. I had a vague image of Episcopalians in sailboats. That was the year I threw up on home plate and walked home from school crying.

Saturday morning recently, at the farmer's market in the dreary armory. A young man in white work pants has bought an extravagant armful of flowers. I smile. He smiles back. May Day mornings in the Irving Park Elementary School auditorium. Peonies, irises, sweet Williams, pansies, and roses in tin cans and Mason jars spread across the waxed wood floor. Garden club ladies arranged bouquets for the sixth-grade girls. I waited in the cool, fragrant half-light, in case they might need some help. They never did.

The young man at the farmers' market and I each searched for the very spot in the outfield where balls

Little League in East Texas

would never land and where you wouldn't be noticed when the teams changed. "Throw it! Throw it!" I'd run as fast as I could with the ball—"Throw it!"—and then heave it (Oh Lord, do I look right?), and it would wobble in toward the diamond. I no longer danced under the trees.

My first role with the recreation department's children's theater was Tweedledum, followed by many princes and kings, since the other boys were even sissier than I. On a float in the Christmas parade, I had to kiss Brenda Kay Huffines's hand all the way down Greene Street to the old train station and back up Elm. Schoolmates jeered.

In 1959, junior high hit. I wonder sometimes what would have happened if I had loosened my grip. Then, annihilation seemed the only option to wrestling with a brutal, faceless future. What if my fears had floored me? As it was, I was twenty years breaking the hold, and only then with the help of another man's strong and gentle arm.

I made A's in social studies because I couldn't throw the football to where Mr. Thompson started measuring from in the phys. ed. proficiency test. I had to win the science fair or Mr. Griffin would smirk at my unmanly lapses. Every time I missed a free throw, I'd shake my head in exasperation or, in later years, shrug comically. Both responses were faked and tore into my muscle and bone. I wanted no part of their sports, neither beating nor getting beat. Seemingly, I withstood the stomach aches, the bad dreams, the anxiety waiting my turn at bat. But my capacity to feel was going. The neurons wore out, and I went numb. In English class, Mrs. Crisp assigned an essay on a familiar emotion: she was startled by mine on hate.

I was elected school president, won awards for service, and prizes for musical, artistic, and theatrical accomplishments, and appeared quite popular. My first week in senior high, I waited and waited for an invitation to join the Junior Civitans or the Key Club, but of course it never came and I was officially out of the running. They knew I was not going to fulfill the destiny of my class and sex. I would never again eat hotdogs with Wesley, Brooks, Jimmy, or Ed, who now wore service club jackets, played football, basketball, or at least tennis, and dated.

In North Carolina, sports attain the numinous, and religion gets right down there on the gridiron and the court. Preachers lard their sermons with basketball jokes, and when they want to deliver a real punch, refer to "muscular Christianity." "Christian athletes" huddle in prayer before football games, and with bull necks bulging at collars and ties, they speak to youth groups. I sat through pep rallies with a few stone-faced friends, and went to none of the games. I wore neither a Duke nor a Carolina button. One Sunday school teacher, a Carolina man, threw me out of his class for talking about conscientious objection.

Music and theater provided refuge for the life-force that had been trampled by physical education. Breathing deep, I swung through Beethoven quartets and Brahms symphonies. I went off to Terry Sanford's Governor's School the summer of my sophomore year, where I, too, was cruel to my ballet-dancing roommate (forgive me, David, brother). My second summer, I lay in bed one night and listened in horror as my roommate Clyde, a baseball star from Shelby, debated in the hall with his friends whether I was queer or not. "Yeah. Well, he's got a girlfriend." Five years later, she would be the first person I told. But music, too, could be made competitive. I was chosen concertmaster of the All-State Orchestra, which meant I'd have to play a solo. I was terrified. Couldn't I be second chair instead? ("Throw it! Throw it!") In the concert my bow wobbled helpless and alone. I decided against music as a career.

Michael Mandrano was from somewhere else. He had long fingernails as well, a peroxided streak, and he *moved* when he walked. In drama class, he talked in a high, exaggerated voice about faraway places from which he'd come and to which he aimed to go. We snickered and led him on. When he entered the auditorium with his homeroom for assembly programs, the general racket exploded into catcalls and whistles. One day, toward the end of my senior year, the catcalls seemed to be for me. I got out just in time.

I escaped to a Quaker college in Pennsylvania. Their pacifism allowed for mandatory football and wrestling. To avoid combat, I tried managing the lacrosse team but got confused keeping score and watching the clock and was fired. I flunked my swimming test and for the rest of the term stood shivering with the other failures by the pool while Coach barked at us. There was nothing sensual about our quaking, bluish bodies. My libido found no quarter (Eros was an unwelcome guest in those puritanic halls), unfinished papers backed up, and I got kicked out. Last fall, ten years later, a college classmate lay in my arms and cried about those years.

Into the maw of the draft. I feared the military as I had feared phys. ed. But unlike my school years, when there was no outlet for my corrosive anger, now there was the antiwar movement. Every Wednesday I stood with the other protesters outside the Federal Building in Greensboro. Once, a car loaded with young men about my age swerved around the corner, and shouts of "Hippycommiefaggot!" clawed at our silence. When the clock on the Jefferson Standard Building finally blinked from "98°" to "1:00," Anne Deagon turned to me and said, "You're the nicest 'hippycommiefaggot' I know." I tried to laugh.

The draft board classified me 1-0; I went off to Boston for two years' alternative service. No longer would I have to dread the orders to run, throw, fight, or kill. When my CO job was over, the first thing to do was come out. Allan and I lay in bed after lovemaking and laughed for joy.

THE LITERATURE OF SPORTS OVERLOOKS ONE IMPORTANT character. The sissie. The traditional foil for masculine bravado, the one who saves all the others from being chosen last. How powerless boys would be without the accusation, "Faggot!" And coaches and drill sergeants. We are the taboo that enforces order, the outside that shapes inside. Outsiders. One night in the early spring a couple of years ago, Carl and I found ourselves on Franklin Street, the main drag in Chapel Hill, the night Carolina was playing the National Championship game. Car horns and sharp voices tore the buzzing air. Word was that victory would see store windows smashed and the streets awash with Carolina blue paint. That we were not visibly queer was slight comfort, and we hurried to get away.

The threat of getting beat up lay just beyond the bruising jostle of football in junior high. There seemed to be nowhere between combat and weakness. Recently, I went to a conference in Norfolk for gay men and lesbians from across the South. Toward the end of a workshop on play for men, a friend said he needed to explore further. He pushed his fists together and frowned. So, locked together in threes first, and then as nine, we writhed on the floor—nine men, black and white, grappling to wrest our bodies and spirits from exile. Afterward, we lay in a sweaty tangle, still and breathing. And then we all hugged each other.

I can dance again now, easy and graceful and strong. Sometimes it's folk dancing with friends, leaving behind the men's and women's parts, dancing wherever we choose. And then sometimes I dance alone.

Out in the barn, shafts of sun slant down from the high windows. A man sways in the quiet light. He turns and turns and turns. He opens his eyes and takes a step. I am almost home.

TWENTY-ONE
Cruising Hatteras

STEVE ROBERTS,
CAROLINE SMITH,
AMELIA MIDGETT,
ANN GREEN, AND
RICK SCARBOROUGH

TWO OF THESE ARTICLES
originally appeared in Sea
Chest *magazine, a project of*
the students of Cape Hatteras
School in Buxton, North
Carolina. Steve Roberts was
born in North Carolina's Outer
Bank in 1901; the other four
writers are all former Cape
Hatteras School students.

Portsmouth
STEVE ROBERTS, WITH CAROLINE SMITH

WHEN OUR DADDIES
were fishing and we weren't in
school, we went fishing with
them. I don't think that I was
over six years old the first time
I went oystering with my
daddy. Children had to work
back in those days, I'll tell you
they did. My brother and I,
we'd cull the oysters and my
daddy'd tong them. I
remember very well that I
weren't big enough that I
could reach the culling tray to
see the oysters to cull them. I
had to get up on the end of
the culling tray to cull oysters.

We started off with a sprit
sail skiff. After a while, it was
an open boat we used in the
wintertime to oyster in and in
the summertime to fish our
pound nets out of. It was
about twenty-one feet long
and about seven feet wide. It
had a jib and washboards on
them. That was for when the
sail would pull the skiff over.
The water didn't come in.

There wasn't any problem

fishing from a sail skiff. If it wasn't blowing too hard, you could fish your net without furling your sail. But there were times you had to furl your sail and lay the sail down inside the boat before you could fish the net.

We children had a lot of pipe dreams about other places our parents would talk about and different things that had happened. We sat on the woodbox where we kept stove wood, and we listened. Sometimes they were only tall tales, but we planted them in our minds. We tell them today mostly for amusement.

They told a tale about a mean sea captain who sailed out of Ocracoke Inlet. The wind died out. He got mad and threw a silver dollar on the floor of the cabin and asked God to give him a dollar's worth of wind. The wind started blowing, and it blew so hard the captain said, "If I had known it was so cheap, I would have asked for a quarter's worth." The story goes, if he had any more money with him, it burnt in Hell.

Those old sailors were mean back in those days. I mean they were mean.

We'd go to one house at night and play the organ and sing and anything we wanted. Most of the music was spiritual music. Once in a while a new song would come down. There was one by the name of "Redwing" that we sang a whole lot. Of course that was just a song, that wasn't a spiritual. The old folks would sit around in their chairs and listen while the young folks played and sang.

In those days they played autoharps. They used to sing sea songs, too. I know just a few lines of one. It went something like this:

It was there by light,
The waters shone so bright,
It put me in the mind of my own
    heart's delight.

Square dances was the word most people wanted to hear. I reckon the song, if it was a song, that was played the most for dancing was "I Danced with the Girl with a Hole in her Stocking." Second was:

Sidney, I went to see my Sidney.
She met me at the door
With her shoes and stockings in her hand
And her feet all over the floor.

The captain of the Coast Guard station would let the man who handled the horses take the wagon—it would take about thirty-five of us to take it across the beach to the strand—and we would have a nice time, just singing and riding. Especially if the moon was full. It was pretty with the moon shining on the ocean.

Cape Hatteras Capers

AMELIA MIDGETT

WE WERE CRUISING ALONG AT A PRETTY FAIR SPEED. THE road was old and full of holes and bumps. It reminded me of being on a roller coaster. The road was also full of curves which, for some odd reason, reminded me of a banana (maybe because of that stupid commercial on TV which shows a man and a woman on a motorcycle following a road consisting of fruits, bananas, etc.).

As we continued on, my friends and I started showing off. The driver started speeding and going in and out of the yellow lines. We were all yelling and carrying on when I looked up and saw dirt fly towards the windshield. I just sat there watching as the ground opened its wide mouth and began sucking the car forward into the center of the earth.

The trees started walking (at least that's what it seemed like to me) towards the path of the car. Bang! We knocked into any tree that wanted to challenge our path.

Then all of a sudden, we ended up in front of this big telephone post. We sat quietly in the car, till finally the driver spoke.

"Is everyone all right?"

One of the girls replied, "Yeah, how about you?"

"All right, I guess," he said, "although my hand and arm feel kinda numb."

Then they both looked at me and I just sat there staring into space. When I snapped back into reality, we all got out of the car, took one final look back and, sunburnt, thumbed towards home.

Friday Night

ANN GREEN

ONE FRIDAY NIGHT WE WERE DOWN BY THE BUXTON campground partying. Kim, Raymond and Randy were all sitting in the van talking. I walked over to them and asked what they were doing. They said, "Just talking." Then they asked me if I needed a ride home. I said, "Yes."

I thought we were going straight home, but we didn't. We went riding on the beach. By 1:00 I was drunk. We were all sitting around drinking and talking. The next thing I remember we were in front of my house and Raymond was opening the back door for me to get out. I got out, said thank you, and stumbled to my front door. My mother opened it and I fell in.

She started yelling at me and asking me who I'd been with. I told her. Then she asked me to let her smell my breath. I walked over to her and blew in her face. I thought she was going to be sick. Then I said I was going to bed.

The next morning I woke up with a bad headache. I dreaded seeing my mother. I got up and walked to the kitchen and got me a glass of Coke. Mom came up behind me and asked if I had a hangover. I laughed and she got really mad. She started yelling and crying, asking me if I was going to be doing this every time I went out. If I was, to get out of her house and go live with my father. So I said I would. I walked to my room and got dressed, then I walked to the phone and told mom I was calling dad to come pick me up. She started crying and I told her I would stay if she would leave me alone. She stopped crying, and I said I would be back later on and walked out.

Fishing Feelings

RICK SCARBOROUGH

I STEPPED ON THE BOAT THINKING ABOUT THE DAY TO
come. It was barely light; the rest of the crew hadn't
shown up yet. This was my first day and I was nervously
excited, wondering if the others were going to make it hard
for me and if I was going to work out.

While I was straightening up the boat they finally arrived.
The boss wasn't in a very good mood. He had pulled a
heavy bender the night before and was suffering for it now.

Getting on the boat without saying a word, they started
her up. The motor let off a pleasant rumble. The fumes
filled my nostrils with early morning air and carbon. I love
the smell.

We got under way and finally the other two started
opening up. I don't know why I was worried, for I had
known both of them a long time. One was even my
cousin.

I was sitting in the bow and they were in the stern
laughing and telling jokes. I heard my name mentioned
over the roar of the engine, so I walked back to them.
Come to find out they were talking about me, mostly I
think because of my age. I was, at the time, the youngest

pound net fisherman around and they were taking advantage of it by teasing me. They were easy guys to get along with and I realized I would be continually teased throughout the season, but I didn't mind.

The nets came in sight and my stomach started churning, like a bug under a rock. As we approached the first one I could see a slick and smell the sweet odor of the fish swimming inside. I jumped down beside the engine and threw it out of gear as we were entering the huge square pound.

When the net started coming to the side of the boat, I had no problem getting into the rhythm of fishing across to the other side. Before we reached the bunt I could see the fish swimming to the top of the water. They were beautiful, every color you could imagine was swimming around within an arm's reach. I grabbed a dip net and started bailing fish into the boat. The other guys were getting a kick out of the way I was going at it with full force and I was enjoying every throw. Soon I was beginning to tire; my muscles were straining with every bail. Then I learned that when bailing out a net you take your own sweet time or you won't last fifteen minutes.

When the boat was full we backed out. It would take a little longer getting home because there was a greater amount of weight slowing us down. I had fish slime on me from head to toe, but I didn't mind. I had always liked the smell of fresh fish and I didn't care if I wore it.

By this time my stomach was churning again, but I wasn't nervous, I was starving. Mike, my cousin, put some fish on the muffler to cook. I could smell the aroma of fresh fish frying, and my mouth started watering. In hardly no time the fish was done and I started chowing down on a nice juicy hunk of bluefish. To my surprise it was great, the best I had ever tasted. By the time we reached the dock my belly was stuffed and I knew I would love this kind of work, and I did, through the whole season.

TWENTY-TWO
The March Became a Riot

D.B., A LEMOYNE COLLEGE FRESHMAN, 1968

I ARRIVED AT CLAYBORN Temple at about 8:50 A.M. because I thought that the march was scheduled to start at 9:00 A.M. However, when I got my sign reading "Mace Won't Stop the Truth," I joined the marchers already waiting in the streets. From the talking, laughing, and waves given by people to familiar friends or acquaintances, I was made to feel that this really was a "holiday march." As I walked along, I began reading some of the signs that ranged from "I Am a Mom" to "Loeb, Kiss My Ass." While standing there in the march looking around, I could see the age level ranged from a baby in a carriage to an elderly lady of about sixty-five. I laughed and said to my sister and Barbara that no one wants to be left out of the parade.

As we stood there, we learned that the march would not leave Clayborn Temple until about 10:30 or 11:00 A.M. At various moments there would be a certain kind of quietness present. At about 9:30 A.M. the whirlybirds (about three) that were flying over the march area were beginning to irritate the marchers. The teenagers from the high school areas began to make up various chants concerning Loeb. However, each time the whirlybirds would come in close, everyone seemed to become angry and thus the whole crowd began to hold their individual signs up and make jeering remarks. I must even admit that the whirlybirds were causing me to become frustrated, because it seemed as though we were in a cage with guardsmen flying over us to keep watch. . . .

As the march turned on Beale Street, the crowd was changing moods. I noticed that hatred was present on the faces of many. I also noticed that they were getting angry because of the policemen lined up and down the street. I also noticed that most of the policemen had somewhat jeering smiles on their faces.

I had just reached Beale and Third when some of the marchers had turned around and said for everybody to go back to the church. This really set the first sparks for violence. A few of the militant marchers present were saying, "No, don't run around, keep marching." I suddenly realized that I didn't know what to do. I had a series of mixed emotions. After my sister told me that she was going on, I decided that I would march on, too. About three minutes later, I heard windows breaking and I noticed that some of the crowd started to run. I headed toward a street that was lined with policemen (about eight), and for a few minutes panic overtook them, because they started running away from the crowd and I noticed that one of them stopped and put his hand on his gun as if to say, "What am I running for, I have a gun." He then stopped and started back toward Beale, and the other policemen that were running stopped and pulled their guns and started going back toward the scene of the violence.

As I was running, I noticed that I had left my sister and I called to Barbara and told her I had to go back. As we arrived on Beale, I saw my sister still standing and looking. Suddenly I noticed that the violence seemed to die down, but I heard a voice coming from a senior at LeMoyne College. He was carrying a stick saying, "Everybody that's scared, get behind me and don't run."

Then everything started again. This time I noticed that the stores were being looted and glass was breaking. My sister and I started running once again. When we got a few feet from Beale, I looked back and could see the police riding down Beale at about seventy miles per hour. I could also see policemen running with their guns in one hand and sticks in the other one. Fear overtook me, and I was trying to find a way home. As I looked around hoping that violence had stopped on Beale, I saw a policeman beat a man until he fell balled up as if lurching in great pain. I also noticed that about three or four policemen ran from their position to get a lick in on the man who was already down. I began to cry and wonder how something like this could happen in Memphis.

Alabama Troopers at Selma Bridge, 1965

As the three of us started walking back toward Beale, I stopped and said we couldn't go because I showed them the fumes from mace and tear gas. However, it was too late to stop. Our eyes began to burn and water. Just as I started feeling sorry for myself, I saw a man coming up the street with his shirt off holding it up to his head. His face was covered with blood and his undershirt was soaked. His

shirt seemed so saturated until it seemed as though you could wring the blood out of it. I began to cry because I thought this was the worst thing that I could see. He stopped a car that was passing by. He didn't know the driver or any of the passengers but he asked them to take him to the hospital. I then made my desperate plea for us to try to get home.

As we started walking toward Beale, the various TV reporters passed us, zooming as if they were in a squad car. We finally made it to Vance Avenue, and I said that the buses were passing people up and that we could go to my grandfather's tailoring shop and wait there until he could take us home. As we started walking near Vance and Third, where his shop was located, we passed a Loeb's Bar-B-Q with two squads of policemen with helmets standing in front, and one was saying that they should get back into their cars and see what the other guys were doing. We knew that he was referring to the other policemen. From listening to him, I felt hard and bitter because I knew that more men like him were down on Beale beating my people and getting sheer enjoyment from beating people. However, we finally made it to our grandfather's shop safely, and we stayed there until about 4:00 P.M.

I feel that the other incidents that I witnessed are too lengthy to put in this one paper, but I would like to say that this was only a sample of the worst that is about to come.

TWENTY-THREE

A New Day Begun

JOHN LEWIS, JIM SESSIONS, AND SUE THRASHER

IN THE WINTER OF 1959–60, the nation was mesmerized by a group of young, black college students in Nashville, Tennessee, who appeared at a segregated lunch counter one Saturday afternoon and asked to be served. All that spring, they filled the jails and the nation with their freedom songs, sparking similar actions and demonstrations across the South. Although an earlier sit-in had been held in Greensboro, North Carolina, it was the small coterie of Nashville students who gave impetus to the concept of nonviolent direct action, and continued to provide critical leadership as the movement spread.

By the spring of 1963, many of the students had moved on to help organize other Southern cities. Still, the Nashville movement persisted. The Nashville Christian Leadership Council (NCLC) held mass meetings regularly, and the local chapter of the Student Nonviolent Coordinating Committee (SNCC) continued to demonstrate for open public accommodations.

Later that spring, John Lewis became national chairman of SNCC. He was in and out of jail constantly over the next few years, and was beaten badly at the Edmund Pettus Bridge in the first attempted Selma-to-Montgomery march. Yet, his commitment to nonviolence never wavered.

John Lewis is now the

189

*director of the Voter Education Project in Atlanta, an organization that
has continued the work of registering black voters in the South. For
John it is a continuation of the work he started in the early '60s, a
movement that has progressed from lunch counter sit-ins to the
attainment of black political power.*

I'M THE THIRD CHILD IN A FAMILY OF TEN. I GREW UP ON A FARM
near Troy, Alabama. When I was four years old, we moved
from where we worked as tenant farmers to a new farm
about a half a mile away. My father had saved enough
money in 1944 to buy 102 acres of land for a little more
than $300; they still live there today.

When we got settled at this new house on the swamp, it
became my responsibility to raise the chickens. At the same
time, I had a growing interest in religion and going to
church so I started playing church with the chickens. This
is the truth—I tried to baptize the chickens, and in the
process, one of them drowned. I felt very bad about it, but
it did not discourage me. I did not lose my great interest in
raising chickens, in a sense, my love for them.

I really don't know where my interest in religion came
from. It could be my family; we all went to a Baptist
church—my mother, my father, most of my first cousins.
My grandfather was a deacon. See, in rural Alabama, we
only had church once a month. So every third Sunday we
would go to a regular church service; that's when the
preacher came. When he wasn't there, we went to a
Methodist church that was right down the hill below our
house.

During that period, when I had a belief in Santa Claus,
one of my uncles had Santa Claus bring me a Bible for
Christmas. It had an impact. And somewhere along the
way I grew up with the idea of wanting to be a minister. It
was well known in the family. One of my aunties would
call me preacher.

I have six brothers and a host of first cousins about my
same age; we all sort of grew up together. It was like a big
fellowship—really an extended family. When we went to
Sunday school and church it was the whole family, not just
the immediate family.

Religion, the whole idea, played a tremendous role in my family. We all had to learn a verse of the Bible at an early age. We *had* to do that. Before meals we had to say grace and then we all had to recite a verse; it's still done even today. On special occasions like Thanksgiving or New Year's or Christmas, my mother or my father or one of us had to lead a prayer.

My interest in the chickens and my interest in the church sort of came together. In addition to helping my family raise the chickens because we needed eggs—it was a necessity, being poor in rural Alabama—the chickens became part of an experiment. I would preach to the chickens each night when they would go into their coop, or what we called the hen house. It was my way of communicating to them. When a chicken would die, we would have a funeral. My younger sisters and brothers and first cousins would be the mourners. We had a chicken cemetery where we buried them and had flowers and everything. I recall a large pecan tree that's still there today; we had a swing and benches under it, and we

would gather there to have the services. People would line
up like they were in church. The service would dismiss,
and we would march off to the cemetery below the house.

THE GRADE SCHOOL THAT I ATTENDED FOR THE FIRST THREE
years was in the Methodist church, just below our house. It
was a public school, but they used the church building.
Next door, there was another one-room school where we
went to the fourth, fifth, and sixth grades. After the sixth
grade, we took a bus to a little town called Banks,
Alabama; I took junior high school in Banks. The high
school was located in Brundidge, going on down toward
Ozark. We passed the white school on our way. We had
this old, broken-down bus. Many of the black families in
this area owned their own land, and the county actually
skipped parts of the road. The area where blacks owned
land was not paved. So, some mornings when there was a
lot of rain, the bus would run in a ditch and we would get
to school late. Or coming from school, the bus would get
stuck in the red mud coming up a hill, and we wouldn't get
home till late at night. That happened on several occasions.

We were very, very poor, like most of the black people
in that area. And I wanted to go to school. I wanted to get
an education. On the other hand, we had to stay out of
school to work in the field, to pick cotton or pull corn, or
what we called "shake the peanuts." From time to time, I
would get up early enough in the morning to hide. On two
or three occasions I actually went under the house and
waited until I heard the bus coming; then I ran out and got
on the bus, so I could make it to school rather than work.
My parents used to say I was lazy, because I didn't want to
stay out and go to the field. But I saw the need and I
wanted to go to school.

WE DIDN'T HEAR MUCH DISCUSSION ABOUT CIVIL RIGHTS.
It was strictly two separate worlds, one black and one
white. When we'd go into the town of Troy, we saw signs,
"Colored only," "White only." The water fountain in the
five-and-ten store. At the courthouse. Couldn't use the

county library. I don't recall hearing anybody speak out
against it. The closest thing was to hear the minister say
something like, "We are all brothers and sisters in Jesus
Christ." Or through the Sunday school lesson, particularly
those lessons based on the New Testament, it came
through: "In Jesus we are one." That had an effect. That
influenced me, no question about it.

In 1955, at the beginning of the Montgomery bus
boycott, when I started taking note of what was happening
there, we didn't have a subscription to the Montgomery
paper. But my grandfather had one, and after he read his
paper, we got it two or three days later, so we could keep
up with what was going on.

We didn't have electricity during those early years. We
didn't get it until much later. We had a large radio, one
with these huge batteries, the kind that have to be knocked
open with a hammer when they decay. There was a local
station in Montgomery, a soul station, black-oriented, but I
don't think it was black-owned. Every Sunday morning a
local minister in Montgomery would preach, and one
Sunday I heard Martin Luther King. Now this was before
the bus boycott. The name of the sermon was something
like "Paul's Letter to American Christians." He made it very
relevant to the particular issues and concerns of the day.
That had an impact. I also heard other ministers on the
station. Our own minister was very aware and talked about
different things.

The bus boycott had a tremendous impact on my life. It
just sort of lifted me, gave me a sense of hope. I had a
resentment of the dual system, of segregation. Because I
saw it. You could clearly see the clean new buses that the
white children had that were going to Banks Junior High
and the buses that were taking white children to Pike
County High School. You see, in the state of Alabama,
most of the black high schools were called training schools.
So in Brundidge, my high school was called Pike County
Training School, and the white school was called Pike
County High School. That was true of most of the counties
in Alabama at that time. In Montgomery, they were saying
something about that dual system.

I remember in '54, the Supreme Court decision, I felt

maybe in a year or so we would have desegregated
schools. But nothing happened. Then Montgomery came in
1955. It was like a light. I saw a guy like Martin Luther
King, a young, well-educated, Baptist minister, who was
really using religion. The boycott lasted more than 300
days; it had a tremendous effect.

During that period, I think it was February of 1956, I
preached my first sermon. I must have been about a week
short of being sixteen. I told my minister I felt I had been
"called"—in the Baptist Church, you hear the "call"—and
that I wanted to preach a sermon. And I preached. I don't
remember the verse, but it was from First Samuel. My
subject was a praying mother, the story about Hannah,
who wanted a child. I've never forgotten the response. I
was really overcome by it all.

From that time on, I kept preaching at different churches,
Methodist and Baptist churches in the rural areas of Pike
County. Churches in Troy would also invite me to come to
preach. I continued to do that until I graduated from high
school in May 1957. In the meantime I had been ordained
by my local church.

MY GREATEST DESIRE AT THAT TIME WAS TO GO TO SCHOOL
—to get an education, to study religion and philosophy.
Somehow, I knew that this was the direction I must travel
in order to become a prepared minister and to be a good
religious leader.

I had a fantastic urge to go to Morehouse College. I'd
heard of Morehouse, and I knew that Dr. King had gone
there. I had my homeroom teacher get a catalogue and an
application from Morehouse. But there was no way. I did
not know anybody. I didn't have any money. It was just
impossible. So this was a dream that was never fulfilled.

My mother had been doing some work for a white lady
as a domestic, and one day she brought home a paper. It
was something like the *Baptist Home Mission,* a Southern
Baptist publication. In this paper, I saw a little notice for
American Baptist Theological Seminary (ABT). It was the
first time I had heard anything about the school. I'm not
sure if it said for blacks or for Negroes or what, but it said,

"no tuition, room and board." And I wrote away. I got an application, filled it out, had my transcript sent up, and got accepted.

So in September, 1957, I went away to Nashville. That was my first time to leave Alabama for any period of time. I was seventeen years old. I'll never forget that trip, getting on that Greyhound bus; it was my first time to travel alone. Nashville was altogether different from rural Pike County, Alabama. It was just another world. I didn't know what to believe. I knew I'd left something and was going to something new.

The school is jointly owned by the Southern Baptist Convention and the National Baptist Convention. It's primarily the financial burden of the Southern Baptists, a missionary school, in a sense, from the whites to the blacks. It was started in 1924, primarily to keep black Baptists from going to the white seminary in Louisville.

I was pulled into a sort of interracial setting. They had white professors on the staff, and white Baptist ministers from the city would come in for chapel. There would be visiting professors from time to time. It was just an eye-opener to go to Fisk to, say, a Christmas concert, and see the interracial climate. I think my resentment toward the dual system of segregation and racial discrimination— probably the tempo of my resentment—increased at that time. Then traveling from Nashville to Troy and from Troy back to Nashville, we were forced to go to a segregated waiting room, to sit in the back of the bus, and all that.

At that time, Little Rock was going on, September of '57. There were many things happening, and because it was an everyday occurrence, I became very conscious of it. I spent a great deal of time during this period preaching what some people call the social gospel. I just felt that the ministry and religion should be a little more relevant. Some of my classmates would tease me about that.

During the summer of 1958, I met Dr. King for the first time. It was in Montgomery. I had an interest in withdrawing from ABT. When I look back on it—and I've thought about it from time to time—it was not just for the sake of desegregating Troy State University. I wanted to be closer to my family, my parents, and my younger brothers and sisters. I could stay at home and go to Troy. I got an application and had my high school transcript and my first year of study at ABT sent there. I didn't hear anything, so I sent a letter to Dr. King, and he invited me to come to Montgomery. I took a bus from Troy to Montgomery one Saturday morning. I met with Fred Gray,* Dr. King, and Rev. Abernathy and told them of my interest in enrolling at Troy State University. They couldn't believe it. They thought I was crazy! But they were interested. They wanted to pursue the whole idea, and we had a good discussion.

I had written the letter to Troy State on my own without talking it over with my parents. I just did it really, didn't contemplate it at all, just sent it in and applied. Later, Fred Gray sent a registered letter to Troy State saying that we hadn't heard anything. We never got any return correspondence. Then the question came up of whether a suit should be filed against the State Board of Education, the Governor and the University. At that time, it would have involved my parents signing that suit, and they didn't want to do it. So we had to drop the whole idea.

I went back to American Baptist in the fall and continued my studies. And then I started attending mass meetings sponsored by the NAACP. The Nashville Christian Leadership Council (NCLC), which was a chapter of SCLC, started sponsoring some meetings on Sunday night at a church downtown.

Later, under the direction of Jim Lawson,† a divinity student at Vanderbilt, NCLC started nonviolent workshops every Tuesday night. For a long period of time, I was the only student from ABT that attended. It was like a class; we would go and study the philosophy and discipline of nonviolence. There was very little discussion during the

---

*Fred Gray was the attorney for Mrs. Rosa Parks, whose arrest triggered the Montgomery bus boycott of 1955 and sparked the organization of the Montgomery Improvement Association. Rev. Ralph Abernathy was then the minister of the Ripley Street Baptist Church.

†Jim Lawson gained national prominence in 1959 when he was expelled from Vanderbilt Divinity School for leading nonviolent training workshops. He later became the pastor of Centenary Methodist Church in Memphis, Tennessee, and played an active role in the 1968 Memphis garbage workers' strike where King was shot.

early workshops about segregation or racial discrimination or about the possibility of being involved in a sit-in or freedom ride. It was more or less a discussion about the history of nonviolence. I did sense that it was going to lead to something; we got into socio-drama—"If something happened to you, what would you do?"—the whole question of civil disobedience. And we dealt a great deal not just with the teaching of Ghandi, but also with what Jesus had to say about love and nonviolence and the relationship between individuals, both on a personal and group basis, and even the relationship between nations.

I remember we had the first test sit-in in Nashville at two of the large department stores, Cain-Sloan's and Harvey's. It was an interracial, international really, group of students. We just walked in as a group and occupied the stools in one area and went to the restaurant, I think, at Harvey's. They said that we couldn't be served, and we got up and left, just like that. It was to establish the fact that they refused to serve an interracial group, or refused to serve blacks. We did one in November of '59 and one in December.

During the Christmas holidays, Bernard Lafayette and I took a bus home from Nashville. Bernard lives in Tampa, so he took a bus as far as Troy with me. I'll never forget it! We got on the bus in Nashville and got near the front. The driver told us we had to move and we refused. He just rammed his seat back, so we were in the front seat right behind the driver all the way and nothing happened. I think when we got to Birmingham, we decided to move. It was a testing period. I don't know why we did it; it was not part of a plan or anything like that.

On February first, 1960, after the sit-ins in Greensboro, Jim Lawson received a call from the campus minister for one of the black colleges in North Carolina. He said, "What can the students in Nashville do to support the students in North Carolina?" Jim just passed the information on.

That call didn't really come to us in a vacuum; we were already involved in a workshop and preparing eventually for a similar action. So, in a matter of days, we called a mass meeting of students on Fisk University campus, and about 500 students showed up. That's when we outlined the plan. It must have been a Monday night. We said on this Tuesday, or that Thursday—we tried to pick T-days since most of the students had light classes on Tuesdays and Thursdays—we would meet at Kelly's church, First Baptist downtown and we would sit-in. We told them that we'd been going to the nonviolent workshop and went through it with them. The people who had been attending the workshops were to be the leaders, the spokesmen in charge of the different groups. We went down and sat in at Woolworth's and Kresge's and other five-and-tens and drugstores like Walgreen's that had lunch counters. It was a quiet day for the most part. That went on for a period of time.

Sometimes we'd sit for two or three hours. We'd have our books and we'd just sit quietly, doing our homework. Someone might walk up and hit us or spit on us or do something, but it was very quiet. The movement during that period, in my estimation, was the finest example, if you want to refer to it, of Christian love. When I look back on that particular period in Nashville, the discipline, the dedication, and the commitment to nonviolence was unbelievable.

Two or three times a week we would go and sit in. And then one particular day—it must have been Leap Year, because I think it was February 29, 1960, a Saturday morning. We met in Kelly's church, and Will Campbell* came to the meeting to tell us he had received information that the police officials would have us arrested and would let all types of violence occur. Kelly came to the church and warned there would be violence. But we said we had to go. We were afraid, but we felt that we had to bear witness. So Jim Lawson and some of the others were very sympathetic and felt that if we wanted to go that we should.

It was my responsibility to print some rules, some "dos and don'ts," what people were supposed to do and what

*Will Campbell was then working with the National Council of Churches in Nashville.

they were not supposed to do: sit up straight, don't look back, if someone hits you, smile, things like that. Several of us engaged in a conspiracy to get the paper and get the rules distributed. At the end it said something like, "Remember the teachings of Jesus Christ, Ghandi, and Martin Luther King: May God be with you." We gave them to all those people that Saturday morning.

Woolworth's was where the first violence occurred. A young student at Fisk, Maxine Walker, and an exchange student named Paul LePrad were sitting at the counter at Woolworth's. This young white man came up and hit Paul and knocked him down and hit the young lady. Then all type of violence started. Pulling people, pushing people over the counter, throwing things, grinding out cigarettes on people, pouring ketchup in their hair, that type of thing. Then the cops moved in and started arresting people.

That was my first time, the first time for most of us, to be arrested. I just felt . . . that it was like being involved in a Holy Crusade. I really felt that what we were doing was so in keeping with the Christian faith. You know, we didn't welcome arrest. We didn't want to go to jail. But it became . . . a moving spirit. Something just sort of came over us and consumed us. And we started singing "We Shall Overcome," and later, while we were in jail we started singing "Paul and Silas, bound in jail, had no money for their bail. . . ." It became a religious ceremony that took place in jail. I remember that very, very well, that first arrest.

Even after we were taken to jail, there was a spirit there, something you witness, I guess, during a Southern Baptist revival. I think our faith was renewed. Jail in a sense became the way toward conversion, was the act of baptism, was the process of baptism.

Then hundreds of students heard about the arrest. We all went to jail and hundreds of others came downtown and sat in. At the end of the day, they had arrested ninety-eight people. During that Saturday night, lawyers and professors and the president of Fisk and other schools came down to try to get us out of jail, but we refused. We said that we would stay in jail, that we felt we hadn't committed any wrong. They wanted to put up the bond. It was not a tremendous amount per person, but altogether it would have been up to several thousand dollars. Finally late that night or early that Sunday morning, the judge made a decision to let us out in the custody of the president of Fisk. And we all came out.

We went to trial the following Monday. The judge wanted the trials separately, but the lawyers objected. They wanted us tried as a group. They tried one case, and the guy was fined fifty dollars or thirty days in jail. At that time, we made a conscious decision that we wouldn't pay the fine, that we would go to jail and serve our term. So we all went back to jail. The next day, Jim Bevel took a group of around sixty to the Trailways Bus Station and they all got arrested. So that was more people in jail. That process kept going on for some time.

I think the older ministers in the community saw themselves in an advisory role. They were leaders of the NCLC in charge of setting up the mass meetings. If we needed something, if there were funds needed to pay a fine or get someone out of jail, we could get money from them. We depended on them for support. They were a resource.

We also got support from the United Church Women and the lady who directed the Tennessee Council on Human Relations, Katherine Jones. A group from the United Church Women would always be on the scene. A lot of times when we were involved in a demonstration in the city, we didn't know that in the store or in the picket line, there were observers from the United Church Women. But they were there, and they were supportive. They came to the courtroom during the trial. They wrote letters and met with the merchants to try to get them to desegregate.

I ONCE DESCRIBED THE EARLY CIVIL RIGHTS MOVEMENT AS a religious phenomenon. And I still believe that. I think in order for people to do what they did, and to go into places where it was like going into hell fire, you needed something to go on. It was like guerrilla warfare in some communities, some of the things people did. And I'm not just talking about the students, but the community people, indigenous people. It had to be based on some strong conviction, or, I think, religious conviction.

I remember on the Freedom Rides in 1961, when we got to Montgomery . . . personally, I thought it was the end. It was like death; you know, death itself might have been a welcome pleasure. Just to see and witness the type of violence . . . the people that were identified with us were just acting on that strong, abiding element of faith.

In Birmingham, we stayed in the bus station all night with a mob, the Klan, on the outside. On the day we arrived, Bull Connor literally took us off the bus and put us in protective custody in the Birmingham City Jail. We were in the jail Wednesday night, all day Thursday and Thursday night. On Friday morning, around one o'clock he took us out of jail and took us back to the Alabama-Tennessee state line and dropped us off. There were seven of us, an all-black group. He dropped us off and said, "You can make it back to Nashville, there's a bus station around here somewhere." That's what he said. And just left us there! I have never been so frightened in my life.

We located a house where an old black family lived. They must have been in their seventies. We told them who we were and they let us in. They'd heard about the Freedom Rides and they were frightened. They didn't want to do it, but they let us in and we stayed there. The old man got in his old pick-up truck when the stores opened and went and got some food. You see, we had been on a hunger strike and hadn't had anything to eat. He went to two or three different places and got bologna, bread and viennas—all that sort of junk food, and milk and stuff. And we ate.

We talked to Diane Nash* in Nashville, and she said that "other packages had been shipped by other means," meaning that students had left Nashville on the way to Birmingham to join the Freedom Ride by private car and by train. We just assumed the telephone lines were always

*Diane Nash was one of the most prominent leaders of the Nashville sit-in movement. She later married Jim Bevel and worked on the staff of the SCLC.

tapped. She sent a car to pick us up, and we returned to
Birmingham and went straight to Rev. Shuttlesworth's*
home to meet the new people. More students from Fisk,
ABT, and Tennessee State had joined the ride as well as
two white students from Peabody. The total number was
about 100.

At 5:30 we tried to get a bus from Birmingham to
Montgomery, and—I'll never forget it—this bus driver said,
"I only have one life to give, and I'm not going to give it to
CORE or the NAACP." This was after the burning of the
bus at Anniston and after the beating of the CORE riders on
Mother's Day. So we stayed in the bus station. At 8:30
another bus was supposed to leave, and that bus wouldn't
go either. We just stayed there all that night. Early the next
morning Herb Kaplow, then a reporter for NBC, came to
tell us he understood Bobby Kennedy had been talking with
the Greyhound people and apparently we would be able to
get a bus later. So we got on the bus about 8:30 Saturday
morning. The arrangement that Kennedy had made was
that every fifteen miles or so there would be a state trooper
on the highway and a plane would fly over the bus, to take
us into Montgomery. An official of Greyhound was
supposed to be on the bus also, but I don't actually recall
that there was one.

I took a seat in the very front behind the driver along
with Jim Zwerg.† On the way to Montgomery we saw no
sign of the state trooper cars or the plane. It was a strange
feeling. For almost four years I had traveled that way from
Montgomery to Birmingham. This time, we didn't see
anyone. It was the eeriest feeling of my life. When we
reached Montgomery, we didn't even see anyone outside
the bus station. We started stepping off, and the media
people began gathering around. Then just out of the blue,
hundreds of people started to converge on the bus station.
They started beating the camera people; they literally beat

*Rev. J. Fred Shuttlesworth, a Birmingham minister, was active in the
SCLC, and president for many years of the Southern Conference
Educational Fund (SCEF).

†Jim Zwerg was an exchange student at Fisk. When the Freedom Riders
reached Montgomery, he was badly beaten and left lying in the street.

them down. I remember one guy took a huge camera away from a photographer and knocked him down with it.

People started running in different directions. The two white female students tried to get in a cab, and the black driver told them he couldn't take white people and just drove off. They just started running down the street, and John Seigenthaler got between them and the mob. Another part of the mob turned on us, mostly black fellows. We had no choice but to just stand there. I was hit over the head with a crate, one of these wooden soda crates. The last thing I remember was the Attorney General of Alabama, serving me with an injunction prohibiting interracial groups from using public transportation in the state of Alabama while I was still lying on the ground. Yes, I was afraid. I was afraid.

YOU KNOW DURING THE WORKSHOPS IN NASHVILLE WE never thought or heard that much about what would happen to us personally or individually. And we never really directed our feelings of hostility toward the opposition. I think most of the people that came through those early days saw the opposition and saw ourselves, really, the participants in the movement, as victims of the system. And we wanted to change the system. People just felt something was wrong.

The underlying philosophy was the whole idea of redemptive suffering—suffering that in itself might help to redeem the larger society. We talked in terms of our goal, our dream, being the beloved community, the open society, the society that is at peace with itself, where you forget about race and color and see people as human beings. We dealt a great deal with the question of the means and ends. If we wanted to create the beloved community, then the methods must be those of love and peace. So somehow the end must be caught up in the means. And I think people understood that.

In the black church, ministers have a tendency to compare the plight of black people with the children of Israel. So, I think we saw ourselves as being caught up in some type of holy crusade, with the music and the mass meetings, with nothing on our side but a dream and just daring faith. . . . I tell you the truth, I really felt that I was part of a crusade. There was something righteous about it.

I really felt that the people who were in the movement— and this may be short-sighted and biased on my part— were the only truly integrated society and, in a sense, the only true church in America. Because you had a community of believers, people who *really believed.* They were committed to a faith.

I was wrong, I think, to feel that way, because you shouldn't become so definitive as to believe that you have an edge on the truth. I think you have to stay open. But, you know, in the process of growing and developing, people go through different experiences.

Interlude

Fat Scrubble (a monster)
CLASS POEM, GRADE 1, MOSSY OAKS ELEMENTARY

He swallows buildings, the universe, the whole planet
His mouth burns up when he drinks the sun like a Coke
He has three heads so he can see everywhere he goes
He has rubberband legs and one plastic leg
He's so round he can hardly hold himself to the ground
Gravity and ropes freeze him there
He's a good monster, for when someone robs the bank
before the thief can get caught he swallows the robber,
*   the building and the money.*

Mr. Sun
CLASS POEM, GRADE 2, SHELL POINT ELEMENTARY

He be hotter than a pot of boiling, steaming orange juice
I'd slap him, knock him in his nose
until my hands swell up and burn.
I'd be blind from the rays.
It would be dark like a thousand nights.
I'd ride my rocket ship home to Earth
where everybody would stare at me, welcome me
Me friends would take me home, fix my hands
take me all around the earth.
And I'd be happy, glad,
like I just been to visit Santa Claus.

Love

SHELIA GUNDER, GRADE 6

When I first fell in love with this boy he was looking at me so hard and I kept looking at him. I said why are you looking at me so hard. He said he liked me. And a scare feeling came through me, and I couldn't hardly say anything but just stand and stare at him. And he ask me what is wrong, and I just open my mouth and said nothing is wrong with me. Then he took my hand, and me and him walked down the road and talked.

TWENTY-FOUR

No. 7 Short Court

MAMIE GARVIN FIELDS

I WAS BORN IN 1888, right here where I am living now, in my great-uncle J.B.'s house. It used to be called "The Parsonage," because Uncle J.B. was a minister of the Methodist Church. Next door were J.B.'s sisters, Lucinda and Harriet; their husbands, Jeffrey Frazer and David Izzard; and their children—Lucinda's children, Thaddeus, Benzina, and Middleton; Harriet's only child, Anna Eliza, whom we called "Lala." Lala excelled in school and was in the first graduating class of Avery Normal Institute. Later she had her own school, which was the first that I attended.

Aunt Harriet had been a seamstress during slavery, a "manshee maker," as they said. She did fine sewing in the Middleton family. One of her jobs was to teach the owner's girls to sew. I remember the little mahogany benches Aunt Harriet kept in her dining room, which she had used in teaching the white girls. You could sit on them. Then beside you were little drawers for your work and for little silver or gold thimbles and scissors, threads, and whatnot. She used those same little benches when she taught us.

Old Auntie had many other fine things besides. When Reverend Izzard came home, he would wash up and change for dinner. Then she would put a beautiful white linen tablecloth on her dining table, which was solid mahogany and had two long leaves that almost reached the floor. She would set it with silver cutlery, which Aunt Lucinda cleaned once a week, big cloth napkins, and colored goblets—the only ones I had ever seen. She would serve from a big troll-foot buffet. Each night Aunt Harriet prepared as if she were expecting the king. Then she called in her husband and all the children, and they would have their meal at the table together.

She was a good-looking woman—tall, slender, and always dressed neatly in her long skirts and apron. Both she and Lucinda dressed well. In those days women wore skirts that nearly touched the ground, with a gathered lace around the bottom under the edge to protect the tail of the dress. The hems were about eight inches and set up pretty, sometimes with crinoline around. They often wore basques, which were blouses that fit tight around the waist and then came on the outside of the skirt. The sleeves were long, puffed at the top and then small down the arm. Sometimes they had lace around the top of the sleeve, around the neck, and down the front. Harriet and Lucinda made these beautiful clothes for themselves. And whenever they went out, they would wear a bonnet and gloves. Both were very ladylike, but Harriet was stern and fearless, while Lucinda, whom we called Sister Much, was sweeter. Sister Much did most of the cooking. She always baked something nice for the children. Old Auntie could be tough. Sometimes the children would run from her.

She used to do what they call social work now. She didn't only take care of her children and her next-door neighbor's (which meant my mother's), she took care of all the children around, it seemed. If they didn't do what Aunt Harriet thought they should, she'd whip them good and then tell their mother what they were doing and that she had whipped them. Many times you could see her bringing children by the hand up to her house. If mothers around the neighborhood lost their children, people would say, "Go on down to Miss Izzard's." Nobody paid her. She'd just take that child out of the sun and bring it to her house. "Don't be walking around in the sun. Go to bed, go to sleep." And the mothers would find them resting or playing on the porch.

LALA WAS EDUCATED TO BE A SCHOOLTEACHER, BUT IN HER time black people could only teach in the country, and even then only in some of the schools. Because she was their only surviving child, her parents were very careful about her. They were afraid for her to go in the country, where she might get sick. So when the time came, Uncle Izzard built her a school in the back of the house—Miss Anna Eliza Izzard's school. He saw that everything was first rate. He made benches and desks, divided the rooms, hung a blackboard—a "modern" thing to have in those days, since most schoolchildren only had slates. And he bought other equipment. Lala kept maps and a globe, schoolbooks of all kinds, storybooks, songbooks, magazines. She had no piano in the school but, when she wanted to teach a new song, she would bring a few children over to my mother's house, where they would use the organ to learn the song and then help her teach the rest of the school. Naturally, most of the cousins were taught by Lala, and many children from around the neighborhood came. Really, she carried on from Aunt Harriet, who was a teacher before her, first to the owner's girls, then in a way to the neighborhood children. By the time Lala started her school, the children were used to coming to No. 7 Short Court. After a while, Miss Izzard's was well known around Charleston and very successful. There was no other like it in Charleston.

At three years old, I got tired of staying home while everyone else went to school, so one day I took over my potty-chair, asking to be allowed to stay. Lala let me sit by her that day, and I was admitted. She gave us a very good basis in spelling, arithmetic, and especially in geography, which she loved. Her geography lessons made us feel we were going all around the world. We knew what rivers we would cross where, when we would have to go over the mountains, what cities we would find. Sometimes we would find the places on the maps or the globe and then look at the pictures in the *National Geographic*. Geography wasn't boring with her, as it is with some teachers. Lala made it easy for us to learn even the difficult foreign names by using songs and rhythm. The same in arithmetic. We learned the times tables with songs. And I can remember her teaching us the Roman numerals by a song and hand claps: "One-i-*one,* two-i-*two,* three-i-*three,* i-*vee*-four," right on up to "M-one-thou*sand!*" Some children in Charleston never learned these at all, but I did before I was six. At six, I went to the public elementary school and made the third grade.

My school had only two black teachers, Essie Alston and Sally Cruikshank, whom Charleston hired just to stay in the law: the Robert Gould Shaw Memorial School for Negro children had to have some Negro teachers. But most of the teachers were white. Two of them resembled Lala in being strict and finely dressed and in remaining unmarried all their lives, but beyond that they were not like her. Sally Walker was short and very stern, never smiled, no warmth at all. If you missed one word in spelling class, you got a caning. Miss Walker was just mean in general.

Another teacher I remember, a Miss Dessisseaux, was from one of Charleston's "aristocratic" white families. Dessisseaux was a Rebel, a pure Rebel! Her job was to teach little children, but it seemed that she couldn't stand the little black children she had to teach. She always walked with an old-time parasol, rain or shine, and used that parasol to make sure you didn't come too near her. If you wanted to say anything to her, she would say, "Come!" and stretch out her arm with the parasol in her hand. When you reached the end of the parasol, which was at the end of her arm, then she would say, "Halt! Right there! Now, what do you want?" Rough, like that. Then you would say, "Miss Dessisseaux, I want to be excused." Then, "Pass!" And that's that. You had to talk to her from that distance, from out there. I can see her now, stiff, very stout, tall, frowning in her long black dress at the black children she had to teach.

Fortunately, we had some nicer teachers, too. There was a Mr. Muller, with an accent, who came from Germany, and Mr. O'Driscoll, who came from Harvard. Because of Boston and the Robert Gould Shaw connection, Harvard sent a good many teachers. You could tell these Northern teachers from our Charlestonians. For one thing, those from the North never punished us like the Southerners did, the cane for this and the cane for that. Those from the South were always beating the children. But Mr. O'Driscoll would punish you and make you learn at the same time. He would send you in what we called the Main Room, so that everyone would know that you weren't behaving. But then he would make you fill up the blackboard with the hardest math problems he could find in your age group. So even though you were ashamed to be in the Main Room, when you came out you knew you had learned something. I always thought Mr. O'Driscoll was an excellent teacher.

Walker, Dessisseaux, and Dixon were the opposite. Miss Dixon was supposed to teach history, but I never knew what it was all about. All you did was read. In the class she would say, "So-and-so, turn to page such-and-such. Read!" When you finished, then she would call the next one. And so on like that. Sometimes you had to commit a certain part to memory. While you recited, she would follow along in the book. If you made a mistake, the cane. And you never could ask a question. I would say I wasn't taught history at Shaw School.

One thing they did drill into us was the Rebel tradition. They had a great many Rebel songs and poems. All had to learn "Under the Gray and Blue" and recite it once a week. The whole school did it, in all the classes. We stood to recite, lined up between the benches and the desks in our classrooms. Then we would sing "Dixie," the whole school, in unison: "I wish I was in de lan' of cotton," in dialect, too. Then they were fond of songs like "Swanee River," "My Old Kentucky Home," "Massa's in de Col', Col' Groun'." This was what they wanted to instill in us. But you never heard these songs and poems at Claflin, which was established by Northerners. And you never heard them at Lala's.

LALA GAVE US THINGS THAT YOU DIDN'T GET AT PUBLIC school, not from the Southerners or from the Northerners. Every Friday we had Bible reading. The children on the back bench, who were the highest in the school, would read, while the rest of us listened. Then Lala would interpret, since the language was hard for us. Right in that little school I learned about the twelve brothers of Joseph;

that beautiful story of Benjamin; about Aaron, whose rod turned into a snake; the story of Moses. We learned to recite certain parts by heart. Lala started us off, so one day we could be Bible teachers in our church schools.

She also liked history. It was from her that I learned about slavery as our relatives had experienced it and what it meant. She told us about her grandfather, who had gone to England as a valet with the Middleton boys; how he studied right along with them and then taught his own sons, Uncle Abe and Uncle J.B., to read and write English, Hebrew, and Greek; how abolitionists sent them to school after the Civil War to become pastors. She taught us how strong our ancestors back in slavery were and what fine people they were. I guess today people would say she was teaching us "black history."

Most of all, she taught us not only to read but to love to read and love to learn. So when Governor Ben Tillman pushed the Jim Crow laws through the South Carolina legislature, although I was just a little girl, I was reading it in the paper. The headline in the *News and Courier* said, "Jim Crow Law Passed in South Carolina." Of course, it got into my head to fight that thing: "I'm a little girl, but I'm going to fight that thing!"

The next morning, early, a white man came to our door and knocked. He had a big bundle over his shoulder. "Is your mother home? I got some things to sell."

Well, although a little girl, I was ready. I said, "Yes, my mother is here, but this is a Jim Crow house and we got Jim Crow money, and we don't buy nothing from no white man! So, now, get away from here!"

Then I ran through the little gate that separated our house from Aunt Harriet's, to head him off before he got to their house. When the man got next door, he was shocked to find that same sassy little girl meet him again. While I was there fussing with the man, Benzina said, "What you doing, Mamie?"

I said, "That white man is here and we are Jim Crow." So then Cousin Ben got on him, too. "We don't want anybody here but Jim Crow people. Go."

Then the man began to say he was not for the law and don't punish him. "I don't like that law," he said. In fact, he was a foreigner and talked with such an accent that it was hard to understand him. (I later knew who he was, though. When I took the Clyde Line ship up to New York, I saw the people at Ellis Island. I thought this peddler must have been one of those who came through Ellis Island down South.) There he was with a big bag over his shoulder, trying to talk to these two black girls yelling about Jim Crow. "Like it or not, you're white," we said. "Now go!" This was the fruit of Jim Crow.

MY MOTHER HAD FOUR CHILDREN TO LIVE AND FOUR TO die. Richard and Maude were very fair. Hannibal and Eva were dark skinned. These were the four who died. Then there were Herbert, Harriet, Ruth, and myself. Herbert was dark and handsome, with soft, black, curly hair. My sisters were both lighter than I was, and Hattie was lighter than Ruth.

It's strange how these skins, these colors, can come along, but they did in our family. My mother was much lighter than all of her sisters, but her brother Richard was about the same color. Uncle George was a handsome fellow! Handsome and black, with straight hair. Mother was light, but her hair was the same as Uncle George's, long and dark. When my sister Hattie was born, the people came from all around to see her, because she was so light and had gray eyes and brown hair, which she kept all of her life. This was from my grandfather Bellinger, I guess, who was a mulatto and looked more on the white side than the black. Grandpa Bellinger had long, light, straight hair, which he wore to his shoulders, like Jesus. Of course, it also came from my white great-grandfather Bellinger. I had to smile one day, in fact, when a friend and I happened to visit the white Bellingers' graves up at Adams Run. A Richard, a Maude, and a Ruth Bellinger all are lying up there: white Bellingers. So our family had not only the same blood but the same names. You could say we learned about integration right there in our house on Short Court.

But we also learned about segregation. When I was a little girl, I recognized that there was a difference, because my brother Herbert used to tease me and call me black—

"blacky-mo"—although he was as black as I was. It used to make me so mad I would almost fight him. He would say, "Well, we are the black ones and they are the light ones. They can do this and that." We used to joke this way, but it wasn't all joke either.

The Jim Crow law made friends into enemies overnight. Our neighbors across the street were the Groens, who had come from Germany. They had two girls and two boys. We were all friendly. This is the kind of friendship we had. When they didn't have sugar, or when they didn't have tea or coffee, they'd send over to borrow some. My brother Herbert was the same age as Kruger Groen, and the two of them would shoot marbles together in the sand between our houses—Short Court wasn't paved then. They would play "onesies" and "twosies," and so forth. Every marble

had a name. When they got tired, they would come over and have lunch.

Now, here comes Jim Crow. The day after, we got to be enemies, and we began to fight each other. That Kruger was always a hotheaded little boy, and he came over to fight Herbert, who was hotheaded, too. The marbles that they had played with on the ground they now used as weapons. Kruger took the marbles and threw over to break the front window; my brother took the marbles and threw back and broke up their windowpane. If you met Kruger in the street, he would call you nigger. Then we would shout cracker back. That quick, the children who had been friends changed.

TWENTY-FIVE

Our Town

NATHALIE ANDREWS AND THE CHILDREN OF THE ROOSEVELT COMMUNITY SCHOOL

*PORTLAND, KENTUCKY, IS
a hard-living little town, rich in
culture and history, but also
fraught with trouble and pain.
Now a pocket of urban
Louisville, Portland sprang up
originally as a crossing place
on the Ohio River, where
travelers had to stop either to
portage around the falls or to
cross the river. Until the
Louisville Canal Company
diverted the waters of the
Ohio, thus directing commerce
away from the falls, Portland
flourished as a river trading
post. Then, one by one, the
old outlying farms were sold
off. Company "shotgun"
housing was erected; factories
and warehouses hemmed in
and defined the area, and the
town became a neighborhood
of Louisville, which had
gradually engulfed it.*

*Portland has strong flavors
of both the river and the
country. You can taste the
river in the drinking water; it
floats in on the floods. But the
country flavor comes from the
people. Many family roots still
penetrate deep into rural
Kentucky. Portland is often the
first and last stop in the
country-to-city migration
pattern, and families still make
frequent visits to their relatives
back in the hills. When asked
what they would like changed
in Portland, many children
wish for more trees and green
things, for it to be more like
the country. The harsh
patterns of urban life still
anger and grieve them. "You
get mad sometimes at people,*

*especially if they stab your cousin or something," says one
eight-year-old.*

*Yet there's a brighter side as well: a strong sense of community
strength and solidarity, a pride in the neighborhood's history and its
institutions. What follows is a portion of a conversation with eight of
Portland's children. All the children are between eight and ten years
old; six are white and two are black. Their names are Dorothy Branch,
John Branch, Michelle Brooks, Sheila Cheatham, Richard Harlow,
Eurana Horton, Ricky Marshall, and Calvin Oakes. The accompanying
photographs are also by Roosevelt students, made through a program
at the school's Portland Museum.*

THE ROOSEVELT COMMUNITY SCHOOL IS A LIVELY AND
valued part of Portland. In the early 1970s, a Neighborhood School Board was formed in the community (under
the Louisville School Board) with real powers to hire and
fire teachers and to evaluate the school's programs.
And the Portland Museum—a special part of the school,
and a strong bridge to the adult world—was created to
help the children discover, uncover and preserve the
history and culture of their neighborhood.

Yet, despite the fact that the Roosevelt Community School has become a model for community involvement admired by school systems across the nation, it has become the target of increasing attacks from the Jefferson County Board of Education. Roosevelt serves a racially balanced population and so is exempt from busing. But the Board of Education charges that the school building is run down and would cost too much to fix. Since 1976 the Board has tried seven times to close the school and bus its students out of the neighborhood. So far, with determined support from the whole community, Roosevelt has weathered these attacks.

WELL, IN THE OLDEN DAYS, THAT HOUSE WE LIVE IN, IT'S still there and we still live in it. I don't think we're ever going to move. We have a picture of our little sister, of my little sister Tracy, running up the steps. She was two years old. She's running up the steps with a little white doggie in her hands. Mom and them took a picture of her.

AND MY GRANDFATHER AND GRANDMOTHER MOVED THERE
and they had my mother, and my mother had Kelly in the
house—in them days when the doctors come to your
house and delivered the baby. She almost died. She was so
small. Mama's lived there all her life. Never moved.

REMEMBER WHEN WE HAD THAT HUNT LAST YEAR FOR A
house that you could shoot a gun through and it would go
straight through the front and straight through the back? We
got that kind of a house. It's like a train house. . . . It's got
three rooms in it. The living room, bedroom, and kitchen
and bath. But, in the living room, we had to put our bunk
beds in there. And one day, I was getting off my bunk bed
in the middle of the night to go use the bathroom. Right on
the first step and my feet slip. I was in the room where the
furnace was. That thing went like a ton of bricks. Yeowww.

And woke up my mom and dad. And then later on my mom moved our bedroom into where their bedroom used to be, and now that's the living room.

OUR RENT-MAN IS A PUNK. YEAH, HE'S SILLY. MY MOM'S been asking for screen doors for the last three years and he hasn't got them up yet. He brung one screen door for the back door and it didn't fit. Then he was going to put it on the side because it just fits. Just that the side door don't have no steps to it. And then you have to step up a step about that high to get in the house. And so he left it and didn't put it up. He left it out back, so my dad put it in the shed, and then he took it back out for he thought it would get too dirty in there. Now it's sitting up on the porch and my mom's been asking for a fence and he got the wood down there and put it in our shed, but he hasn't put our fence up yet and she's asked for that two years ago.

I'VE LOTS OF SISTERS AND FOUR BROTHERS, COUNTING MY dead one. And they all live at our house except my sister

and my brother and my other sister, and they fight with me a lot. But I have to tell my mom, and she whips them. My two big sisters, they sleep in a room, and me, my brother, and my other sister, we sleep in a room. Sometimes we fix up the rollaway bed and we sleep on the couch. We sleep on the chairs and we sleep anywhere. Well, I sleep with my mom sometimes, and when my dad's home, I don't sleep with them. But, when my dad's not home, I sleep with her sometimes.

WE'RE HAVING NINE PEOPLE OVER TO OUR HOUSE FOR Thanksgiving. My mother put the menu up this morning. My grandmother's fixing chittlings. My mother's fixing ham and turkey. We're having potato salad, macaroni and cheese, deviled eggs. We're having Kool-Aid for the kids and tea for the grown-ups.

ONE TIME, I WAS REAL SMALL, AND I WANTED A DOLL AND I was by my grandmother's house. My mother said she wasn't going to get me one. I told my grandmother that,

and she said, "Go lie down for a little while, baby. When you wake up, you'll have a doll." When I waked up, she had made me a little doll herself.

MY GRANDPAW DIED IN A CAR ACCIDENT. HE WAS COMING back off the expressway to get some more wood for the house, and there was two people on each side of him. They was drag racing on the expressway and he was right in the middle of them, and they hit his car. They rammed into him and his car went out of control, and he went into the wall and died. . . . I don't have any grandfather.

MY MOTHER SAID, WHEN I GET OLD ENOUGH, IF I WANTED to, I could live in the country, because she says she might be moving to the country because it's a little quieter. We live by the expressway and we hear all the traffic noise.

MY DAD WORKS AT LINKER'S BAKERY AND SO DOES MY uncle and so does my other uncle. My aunt used to but she don't. They make buns and stuff. My dad messes with the dough and puts it in a machine. He's been there about sixteen years. My mother used to work down there on Crittenden Drive at this printing company. She worked, but we stayed with our aunt until she got off. She can't work now because she's having another baby.

DAD WORKS IN A MILL. HE RUNS A BIG OLE MACHINE. HE makes it go round and round, and he wraps the spools up. Some of them are about five to seven thousand pounds. Thirteen thousand pounds in two of them. This one man, this colored man, he tricked them. I believe his name was Mozeek. And he heard one of them things go, and he wasn't hurt. That man was lying down on the ground and groaning and moaning. And then my dad came over there and saw him and saw that he wasn't hurt. He done scared him to death.

MY DAD IS A FIREMAN, AND I'M GOING TO BE A DOCTOR.
My mom is a housewife. Dad's been a fireman nineteen
years and he really likes it. Sometimes he takes us to the
firehouse and lets us go in a fire truck and gives us a Coke.
And he goes to Shamrock's every time he gets off work.
He don't come straight home. He goes to Shamrock's for
four or five hours, then comes home to eat supper and
goes back to Shamrock's.

SHAMROCK'S IS A NICE PLACE. PEOPLE'S SUPPOSED TO FIX
the upstairs up and move in. Then Nemar might sell the
upstairs and make them a doorway. . . . He lets me play
pool and stuff. . . . Some of them buy me stuff, me and my
friends and my cousin, about twelve people. No women
can come in. Last time they let women come in, they were
looking for their husbands. People got in a fight in there
and stuff, and then they tore the place up, so they had to
put a sign up, "No Women."

SHAMROCK'S IS, I DON'T KNOW, TWENTY-FIVE YEARS OLD.
People used to live in it. It's got signs hung on it. Great big
old whiskey bottle that says Seagram's Seven on the side.
Then it gots a sign out front with .22 bullet shots in it. Guys
had a gunshot fight. Hit the sign. Me and my friend John
Ryan might get Shamrock's when we grow up. We just
gonna leave the same signs up or else get some new ones
just like it. We was going to leave all the trophies in there.
. . . Well, they got basketball trophies. Trophies hanging up,
pictures of horse races, football helmets, long-time-ago
football helmets. They got one worth $200.

LANNAN'S PARK IS NAMED AFTER MY GRANDFATHER, AND HIS
picture is in Nelligan Hall, and we got a picture of him at
home with some other people. My grandmother and my
mom, she goes to Nelligan Hall on Fridays and Saturday
meetings there. My aunt Katie, my mom's sister, she has
the key to the place. And she's got a key to the little bus,

and we go camping in summer. You can take a whole truckload for a dollar and a quarter, if you can get them in.

SEE, NELLIGAN HALL, IT'S OPEN TO THE PUBLIC. WE HAVE bingo there on Saturday and pinochle and playing cards on Fridays at seven, ending at one or two o'clock in the morning. See, it's not for little kids, it's just for adults. But we can play bingo and stuff. See, my brother, he won, let me see, $100 there once. Then he won $20. And one time I won $29 there. Well, we had a party over there for my cousin Mary Lannan. See, 'cause she's going to the army.

WE'VE GOT A CLUB AND A CLUBHOUSE. WHAT'S THOSE things where you call a spirit? We had one of those. We couldn't pronounce the name. We forgot what the name was. We had one of those. We was down in our club, down this block. So we said, "Terry, if you're here, tap us on our shoulder and make something fall in the club." And we turned around and the whole table fell. It stands this tall, and that thing just fell over to the ground. We were in the backyard, and we said, "Terry, if you're here, make a noise." And I swear—am I lying, Nathalie?—something said, he said, "Don't-you-go-back-in-that-club." Come on, something said that. Scared us. We took off running out front. I didn't believe in that stuff until yesterday. Something said, "Don't-you-go-back-in-that-club." We were all shaking yesterday.

TWENTY-SIX

Mill Village Memories

VALERIE QUINNEY

CARRBORO, NORTH Carolina, was typical of many Southern Piedmont mill villages at the turn of this century. The mill owner, Tom Lloyd, was a local man who had made his money through farming and through small farm-related enterprises (a grist mill, a saw mill, a cotton gin). Carrboro itself was built largely by Lloyd to house the workers in his mill. He built the mill in the 1890s, during the great spurt of growth in the Southern textile industry. The workers, descendants of British settlers in the area, came in from nearby farms. The mill's overseers were chosen from the ranks of the workers, and as a result, owner, overseers, and workers were all linked by shared community and church ties, if not by direct kinship.

Among the mill workers were many children, whose labor was seen as necessary for most families to survive. Children went to work in the mill as early as age six; some at eight or nine; most by the time they were twelve. Work at the Carrboro mill meant twelve hours a day, five and a half days a week.

In 1974, thirty Carrboro men and women—all of whom passed their childhoods in the village before World War I— participated in an oral history project under the auspices of the Chapel Hill Historical Society. Their memories illuminate the hard work and bad times, the vibrant strength of family and community, the games and the chores, and the social pastimes which shaped a child's life in this mill town eighty years ago.

FOR A SMALL CHILD, THE VILLAGE WAS A WARM AND friendly place, with narrow perimeters which were easily mastered. A child could walk independently wherever he or she wanted and soon knew by sight almost the whole population. Out of necessity—store-bought toys were rare —they used their imaginations to devise their own games and to create playthings out of natural objects. The woods began where the backyards ended and offered a wide and stimulating world for children to play in. They spent hours creating their own minuscule houses and farms. They covered rocks with green moss to make "upholstered" furniture. Small pinecones became the chickens in the yard. The children used bugs for pets and took them on walks to the store, harnessed with pieces of thread. Corncobs, dressed in scraps of cloth, became the people, and they rode around in boxes, which served as wagons, to visit other corncob people. When a death occurred in a corncob family, one of the boys would preach a funeral sermon, and all the children would join in "Rock of Ages," singing through their tears. All would be decked out in their best hats, made of oak leaves woven together with broomsedge and decorated with daisies. On these and other occasions, the children would feast on wild blueberries, strawberries, blackberries or nuts, as the season offered.

The woods were also a perfect place to play "Indians" and to satisfy a craving for mystery and adventure. One woman we talked to recalled a special enchanted afternoon:

One day we wandered off just a little farther from home. There was quite a crowd of us. And we just kept a-walking, and kept a-walking, and we came upon something that was buried in the ground. And we could tell from the way it was sticking up that it was a handle of something, or maybe a handle to a pitcher. Just the way it was sticking up. And it was a kind of copper color. And I won't ever forget it! We was so thrilled we didn't know what to do. And we all—you know how a pack of children will say—we figured it was Indian, something that the Indians had buried back there. Well, instead of us marking the place where it was, we all run home to tell our parents about finding it. And they went back with us and we never did find it. We never did find out. And I've often wondered about it, after I grew up!

ANOTHER GREAT SOURCE FOR A CHILD'S BUDDING imagination was the long sessions of storytelling that took place at home, around the fire in winter or out on the porch during the long summer evenings. Boys and girls would come from all over the village to hear the scary ghost stories that a certain pair of old ladies loved to tell. They sat on the porch on summer evenings, and their stories were so deliciously frightful that the boys and girls were afraid to walk home down the road.

Some of these stories were not just made up for fun, but were based on "real" experiences with the supernatural. Older relatives told of meeting spirits and portents by the side of the road on dark nights:

My aunt was telling about one night she was going home. She was going through the woods, and beside the path, she said, was a little lamb, just lying there. And she wondered where the little lamb came from, because nobody around had sheep. And she said she thought, "Well that was odd." But she went on home. And the next day she went back to see about it, and there was no lamb. There was no sign of it ever having been there or anything. And she thought it was a ghost.

The Devil figured prominently in many of these tales, and in the children's fears. One child was certain she had met him:

I was always awake when the rest of the family was asleep. And scared to death sometimes. I know one night somebody knocked on the door; everybody was asleep but me. And I went to the door, and there stood the blackest man I ever saw with things with gold spots on them. And I thought, "Oh, my Lord, there's the Devil." And it was a dark night.

Later, she realized he was a peddler selling picture frames that were painted black, flecked with gold.

It was said that a person's destiny was governed by unseen forces. People always planted their gardens on Good Friday to prevent evil from befalling them—all except the potatoes, which had to be put in on a dark night in March. They killed their hogs on the waxing, not the waning, of the moon. Women hoped that their babies would be born during the full moon. On New Year's Day people ate black-eyed peas and hog-jowl for luck; they also avoided washing clothes on that day lest a death should occur in the house during the new year. One woman talked about her two aunts and the various precautions they took against bad luck:

If they were in here and started out to go somewhere and forgot something, they stopped out there and made a cross-mark and spit on it. Because it would be bad luck. If they would come to see you and went in at one door, they went back out that door; they wouldn't go in one door and out another door. And Aunt Susan used to tell us if our feet went to sleep to wet our finger and make a cross-mark and it would stop.

Often the grown-ups would invoke the supernatural as a form of discipline. Like their ancestors in England, people would warn their naughty children that they'd better be good or else the "Bugger Man" or "Raw Head and Bloody Bones" would come and get them. One woman recalled:

I remember one nightmare I had. Old Raw Head and Bloody Bones came out and threw my brother in the fire, and my brother got out and threw Raw Head and Bloody Bones in the fire. I can't even remember how Raw Head and Bloody Bones looked! But he ran under my bed, and oh, for weeks I was afraid to pass that bed. I guess I was five years old then. And I know a nephew of mine came along. They told him the story of Raw Head and Bloody Bones, and one day he went down into the garden, and during the night the dogs had dragged up an old cow's head. That little fellow saw that, and he screamed bloody murder. It was a raw head and bloody bones.

There were also historical tales—personal stories centering around family or community events but also often caught up in the larger skein of regional, even national, history. Children heard a great many stories from the Civil War, at that time less than fifty years past. One woman said her father talked often about the Battle of Gettysburg:

My daddy served in the war for four years. And he got shot through both hips. He said he stayed in a little old log cabin they had for a hospital. And they put a bucket of water over him and drove a tiny little nail hole so it would just drip. That's all he had done to him, was that water dripping into that bullet hole, till the fire got out of it. He said that when that water would give up there, he'd scream like murder. He still stayed on in the service, till it was over with.

Another woman remembered hearing many times the story of her uncle's death in the war; the family did not know he had died until a wagon carrying his body turned into their drive. One narrator brought out a child's dress and a tiny gold ring which had belonged to her mother and had been buried along with other family treasures to be saved from the invading armies. The moral of most of these tales seems to have been that a strong family can get through the hardest times.

Other stories stressed the importance of hard work and thrift. Tom Lloyd, the mill owner, was often pointed out to the children, and his success was always attributed to his penny-pinching habits. Every child in the village knew, for instance, that if Tom Lloyd ever saw anything lying on the ground—even something as small as a pin—he picked it up and saved it. They also knew the story about Lloyd and the salesman who came to town on a train:

Watermelon Time in the Village

Tom Lloyd was over at the depot one day. He was there with them old dirty overalls on and was filthy. Firing the boilers and things like that all the time there with wood. And this here salesman come in, he's all dressed up, a nice-looking fellow. Said he'd give somebody a quarter to carry his suitcase over to the office. And Lloyd was standing there; he said, "I'll carry it over there." And he run on over there and set it down. And the salesman said, "I come here to see Tom Lloyd." He said, "I'm Tom Lloyd." But he done got his quarter.

One father often told his children this story about his childhood: as a small boy, he spent a lot of time picking strawberries and blackberries with his mother and brothers and sisters. Then he would walk five miles into town to sell them, sometimes even making two round trips in a day. One day a storekeeper who had just bought some of his berries saw the little boy staring at a display of Barlow knives.

And he said to him, "Little boy, would you want one of
them knives?" He said, "Yes, sir, I would love to have
one, but, Mister, I haven't got no money. My mother
makes me bring my money back to live on." And [the
storekeeper] says, "Well, what about this now; I'll let you
have that knife, and you may pay me so much a week.
Go home and ask your mother if you can do that. Ten
cents a week or just as much as you want to."

The storekeeper followed him to the door and patted him
on the head and said, "Now, little boy, your credit's all
you've got, and when that's gone, you won't have
nothing."

Besides the stories, children absorbed a storehouse of old
sayings. Along with reinforcing the community values of
hard work and thrift, the sayings tickled the children's
fancies. A favorite was "You can get used to anything but
hanging." Another cautioned, "Be careful what you pray
for, you might get it." A wife was often praised thus:
"When she put her finger on a penny and raised it up,
there would be a nickel there." Thus, even at a very young
age, children were already absorbing the values which
would help to sustain them through a lifetime of hard labor
in the mill.

The same parents who passed on to their children such a
rich heritage of spoken family and community history told
them virtually nothing about the meaning of two central
family events: sex and birth. One woman talked about her
childish ideas of where babies came from:

I was six years old when the youngest child of the family
was born. I had an aunt that came with her suitcase, and
she came before to stay until it was time for the baby.
Then she was going to stay afterwards till my mother got
able to get up. Well, I thought all the time that she
brought the baby in that suitcase. I was six years old, and
I mean I believed that for a long time after that. Because
we just didn't know things back then.

Reticence about sex, birth, and death was a way of
protecting small children from discussions they couldn't

understand—but they learned about those experiences anyway.

They also learned, very early, the structures of race relations in the community. Black people lived in separate areas of the village, and several people remembered that blacks did not venture into the village center after dark. They did not work in the mill except in menial jobs; they did not go to the same churches. White children in the country might meet black children at the spring and play with them, but this did not happen in the village.

Nevertheless, the narrators in our project did speak of individual black people who had touched their lives in some way. When a mother was sick or died, families often hired black women to take care of the house and the children; they would usually sleep with one or two of the small children and take their meals with them. A black woman called Aunt Cindy Atwater raised one such family of children. They remember being cuddled and comforted; one woman recalled, "I loved her like a mother." She told them stories about her life in slavery and just after the Civil War:

She'd tell about the Ku Klux coming through, and about Master. If he heard them singing—they'd just try to have prayer meetings and things like that—and if he found it out, he'd just go down there and beat them and treat them terrible.

As much as tradition, children were taught skills. In the summertime, small children went with their mothers to pick berries, to be exchanged at the store for precious items like sugar. They also tended the garden and helped in family cash-raising efforts. One of these was making little sacks to hold the tobacco people used in rolling their own cigarettes:

The tobacco sacks were bagged up in these great big sacks and piled up in the Sack House, and then we would go and get them. We had to clip little squares; then we had to turn them. We had a wire fixed on a board. We had to turn them, and then we had to string them. Then after we strung them, we would have a party, a sack time, and invite all of the neighbors. And in that way, we helped each other with the sacks. After they were tied, then they had to be stacked, twenty-five to a stack, and they had to be packed. After we'd gotten that done, we'd carry them back to the Sack House and we got our pay. Well, in what time I wasn't playing, I would help, you know. I never will forget, one summer, whenever my mother and father got the money, they said, "Well, you made a dollar." I don't reckon I was over seven or eight years old. But I went with my mother to town. I told her that I wanted to spend my dollar for something that I really wanted, and I bought me a pair of Mary Jane patent leather shoes.

Both men and women had to use all their ingenuity to help the family survive on the low mill wages, and their children helped. Women and girls made all the family's clothes and often sewed for other people. They sold eggs to the store. If there was an extra bed in the house, they took in a boarder. Men and boys trapped muskrats and sold the pets. Sometimes, if a man had managed to hang onto the family farm, he and his boys would go out there and cut oak trees to sell to the railroad for cross-ties, or cedars to sell to the cedar mill, or firewood to chop up and sell in town.

At home, as at work, the divisions of labor between the sexes were strict and clearly observed. Men might cook, but they did not wash dishes, or do the laundry, or sweep or make beds. Men could milk, but it was the women's job to churn. Men did not bathe the children, but they could take them swimming in the creek. Women sewed and washed and ironed; they cooked and put up food for the winter. Men butchered hogs, chopped wood for the stove, tended the garden, and caught fish to augment the family's food supply.

Chores for boys and girls were structured accordingly. Boys cut the grass, chopped firewood, and fetched water from the well. Boys and girls over five years old watched younger ones in the yard; either sex could be sent on errands to the store. After they turned eight or so, girls began washing the dishes and the clothes. Girls cleaned the house, helped with canning and preserving, and learned to cook and sew. One woman recalled that as a little girl she ironed her five brothers' shirts with big, heavy flatirons, heated on the wood stove. She also milked the cow, made the butter, and cooked for the whole family while everybody else was working in the mill.

Oftentimes the "whole family" included more than just the mother, father, and their children. Young, unmarried cousins might come from the country to live with their relatives while working in the mill. Sometimes an elderly relation came to live:

Back then you never heard tell of nothing but a poor home. There was no rest home. We heard tell of a poorhouse; that's what it was called. But there was none of my people ever went to one. I had two aunts that lived with us. When their husbands died, my Daddy, their brother, took them in, and they was two of the family.

That made thirteen people in a five-room mill house: mother, father, nine children, and two aunts.

There was a bed sitting under a flue. And there was a bed in this corner. I slept with one of the aunts. And two of my sisters slept on the other bed over here. The other aunt and my little brother—oh, I reckon he was about five years old—slept in the bed under the flue.

Even when there were no other kin living in the house, children were close to a wide extended family reaching throughout the village. One woman told us that her favorite spot as a child was her grandfather's blacksmith shop, where she basked in his attention and that of his customers. Another recalled escaping from her strict, "fussy" mother's household to play at her cousins':

Aunt Lilly, she was sick a lot, and she had a whole bunch of children. She let them do just any which way they wanted to. We all had the biggest time when we were over at that place, because nobody held any restrictions.

We played in the bed upstairs, dressed up in the wrong clothes, which my mother did not allow.

This woman described her mother as smart but hard on her children and vowed to be a different sort of mother herself:

I thought if I ever got grown and had children, I'd let them go their own way. And I never did stop my children from playing, because I'd been deprived of it all my life. If I played any, I had to get leave of absence and go somewhere else.

Only the most candid of our narrators spoke of hard feelings between family members. One woman said, "My father never took up much time with any of his children. I never knew my father very well. I never cared too much for him." Conflict among members of the extended family was rarely mentioned either, and then only in passing. One woman remarked, "Uncle T. didn't think too much of some of his brothers, but he treated them all right." Rather than resent the fact that their homes were often crowded with relatives, boarders, and small children, people placed a high value on each member's contributions to the group's survival. The work required simply to get through each day was so arduous that getting along became a necessity rather than an option.

Since most children went to work in the mills at age twelve, the village school lasted only seven grades. If students wanted to go to high school—and their families could afford for them not to work—they had to go to the high school in nearby Chapel Hill and face the challenge of trying to mix with the children of the professors at the University of North Carolina. Two women recalled their brother's experience. "He went to high school down there, and he quit because the Chapel Hill people would say, 'Don't get close to him, you will get lint on you.'"

Most Carrboro children, however, counted themselves lucky to get through seventh grade. The curriculum at the school was traditional, emphasizing the basics: reading, writing, arithmetic, history, geography. As was common in those days, the school put on a special program at least once a year in which each child got up and spoke a piece, or sang, or acted a part before an audience which included most of the town.

Most of our narrators remembered their teachers as being kind, especially in the early grades. One woman recalled her teacher's tact during the hard first day at school:

I never will forget the first day that I went to school. Every time I saw my mother come to the well, I raised my hand to be excused. I hated to leave her so bad that I didn't know what to do. I wanted to go to school; if she hadn't come to the well, and I hadn't seen her, I would have been all right. But I was in the first grade. I just couldn't stand it unless I went out and talked to her a little bit. Then she would go back to the house with a bucket, and I'd go back in school. The teacher, she caught on to what it was. She always pretended. She knew where I was going.

Discipline soon became strict, though; if a student got whipped at school, he or she was sure to be whipped again at home as soon as the parents found out. In school, as at home, however, the mere threat of a whipping was usually effective.

After the Carr family bought the mill in 1909, they started a night school for the children who had to work in the mill during the day. The children went to school from six till nine at night. But the experiment didn't last, since the children had many chores to help with at home after work and were also generally too tired to concentrate.

FOR MOST CHILDREN, THEN, SCHOOL—LIKE THE REST OF the small child's freedoms and privileges—ended when they went into the mill. Until 1904, North Carolina (like other Southern states) had no laws at all regulating child labor. The state legislature passed a law that year setting a minimum age of twelve years and also restricting people under eighteen from working more than sixty-six hours a week. But this law remained mostly theoretical until well after World War I, because of lack of inspection and enforcement personnel.

The Carr family opposed hiring children under age twelve and pressed for a law to provide for factory inspectors. But the reality for most mill families was that a father could not support a wife and children on his wages. The United States Bureau of Labor conducted a study in 1907–08 which revealed that only 30 percent of cotton mill families in Georgia, South Carolina, and North Carolina had what could be termed a "fair" standard of living. Twenty percent were living below the "minimum" standard; they did not even make enough money to provide adequate food and shelter. The father's wage *had* to be supplemented by the wages of his wife and/or his older children.

A young couple with one child could arrange their working lives without too much difficulty; a neighbor or relative could usually be found to keep the child while both parents worked. But a mother with several small children found it impossible to work at the mill while also caring for the children, cooking, cleaning, and doing the laundry and other endless tasks of maintaining a large household. Unless there were aged relatives living in the home and able to help out substantially, the mother had to quit her job in the mill. This put a growing family under severe financial strain, until the oldest child began earning money at the mill. When the youngest child grew old enough to be still and quiet beside her, the mother went back to work, too, taking this child with her. Many of our narrators recalled going to work with their parents or older siblings; often these young children would do simple tasks—turning the stockings inside out, for instance—for no pay.

The Carrboro mill had two floors—one for spinning cotton thread, the other for knitting cotton stockings. Both floors were lined with big machines. The building was heated adequately in the winter but was almost unbearably hot in the summer. No fans were used because they blew the lint around and broke the threads. The whole inside of the mill was filled with lint. The nature of the work required constant squinting to keep track of the fine threads. The only drinking water was kept in a bucket and the dipper shared by all the workers (hence, the rapid spread of influenza through the mill during the epidemic at the close of World War I). Not until after the war was a toilet installed inside the building; until then, people had to go to the outhouse that sat by the railroad tracks.

Nevertheless, most of our narrators said they had wanted to start working. As small children, they had looked forward to the new status their wages would bring them, and they knew that their income was really needed. One woman told us about her entry into the mill at age eleven and her disappointment when the mill owners later decided she was too young:

They said that I couldn't come in and just help. I would have to be on the payroll so they put me on the payroll. And I worked there, I don't know how long—several months—and then when they came over, they said I couldn't work unless my father signed me up for being twelve years old. Well, he wouldn't do it. He said he didn't want me to work no way then. But I wanted to work. When they put me out of work, I cried. I didn't want to go to school. I just wanted to work and make some money. I just thought I was doing something, I reckon.

Sometimes little children looked forward to going to work because other children were there and the atmosphere was friendly and familiar. The overseer was from the village; all the children knew him, and he generally treated them gently. One woman, born in 1901, began working in the mill when she turned six. She made about twenty cents a week. For a while after she started working, she still needed an afternoon nap:

They'd have piles of those stockings, and they smelled good, like new cotton. I always couldn't go to sleep overnight, and during the day I'd get so sleepy, and I'd crawl up on that pile of stockings and go to sleep.

Another narrator recalled nailing the overseer's Sunday shoes to the floor and watching him slip his feet into them at the end of the day and try to walk. This same person was afraid of thunderstorms and ran away from the mill one day when a big storm came up:

My mother said, "Mr. Johnson, I don't think that she will go back. She's scared to death of thunderstorms." He said, "If you will just come back and go to work and if another thunderstorm comes up, you can quit and sit down, and just as long as it takes, I won't expect you to work."

A Kid's Life in Carrboro

BY THE TIME THE CHILDREN WERE TWELVE, THOUGH, THEY had become regular full-time members of the work force. Like the grown-up workers, they got up at five o'clock every morning when the mill whistle blew. Boys helped feed the livestock and the chickens and milked the cows; girls cooked the breakfast and washed up. Then it was off to the mill for twelve hours. In the cotton thread department, girls generally worked with the spools that wound the thread, while boys changed the bobbins on the spinning frames or packed the yarn in boxes. On the knitting floor, young girls often worked as "toppers," fixing the stocking tops onto the machines which sewed them onto the rest of the stockings.

But in talking about their mill work, our narrators did not dwell on the long hours of tedious, eye-straining work or on the many miles they walked each day up and down the spinning frames. The social scene was uppermost in their minds, just as it is with most teenagers.

Yes, we talked. You could talk. The spinning frames, oh, they were long. And like mine was here, somebody's over here, and somebody's over there. We would catch up with our work, and then we would go sit down and talk. We had a good time.

They also learned that getting along together was as important in the mill as it was in their homes. The machines were difficult to run and often balky; the workers depended on one another to keep them running smoothly and to avoid losing pay because of wasted time:

You had to watch to keep one spool from blowing over and getting tangled with the other one. You'd just make a mess of them. And every time you made a mess, you lost so much time on it, getting it straightened out. Most of us were right good to each other. If anything happened—you didn't thread it up just right—if anybody else saw it, they'd run and stop it for you. So it wouldn't make too big a mess.

When the mill's whistle finally blew again at the end of the day, there was still supper to be cooked and chores and housework to be done. This meant that the only free time that the working children had was on Saturday afternoon and Sunday, and much of that was taken up by the endless chores around home. In the few free hours that remained, the adolescents, like the younger children, devised their own entertainment.

The boys' first love was baseball (from which girls were excluded). They also hunted and fished and went swimming in the creek. Unknown to parents and the preacher, the boys also had a secret cave where they gathered to shoot craps. Another favorite, and also illicit, pastime was jumping onto the boxcars of the train as it passed slowly by the Carrboro depot:

I don't know how the engineer knowed we was there, but he stopped the train and told us if we was going to ride that train to get in the coaches like we were supposed to be or we'd fall down and get killed. He knowed my daddy mighty well, you know; they were good friends.

The boys engaged in rougher, uglier games as well, including some violence along the lines of race and class which marked the community. They sometimes threw rocks at black boys; one narrator recalled an incident in which a black boy was seriously injured. The Carrboro boys also harassed—and sometimes even beat up—any university boys who came to visit the village girls.

Theft, however, was rare. In 1900, the whole township was served by one constable, and he got very little business. One narrator recalled this scene from his boyhood:

Used to, down at Albert Lloyd's store, us boys would sit out there at night in the summertime and some of the wintertime, depending on what the weather was. He never carried no apples or no bananas or nothing in at night. They hung out there. We'd sit out there and talk till pretty late at night sometime, and nobody didn't borrow none of them apples and oranges out there. They didn't think about borrowing none.

The girls were kept closer to home. They liked to gather at someone's house and crack nuts and make candy. In the summertime, they would make ice cream.

Girls often went walking together. One narrator recalled how she and her sister walked three miles out into the country to visit some relatives. They spent the night, and during the evening it snowed. Next morning, they walked home again as the sun shone on the new snow. "A beautiful day," she said.

MANY PEOPLE IN THE COMMUNITY FROWNED ON CARD playing and dancing, although some families engaged in both, and farmers on the edge of town sometimes held dances in their barns. These mores grew from and were enforced by the other social institution in Carrboro (besides the mill)—the church. There were two in the village, one Baptist and the other Methodist. Memories of individual ministers were vivid. One woman praised the minister at her childhood church, saying, "He always made me feel important," and this sentiment was echoed by several others. Both congregations were small, enabling the preachers to know and speak to each child as a special individual. The easy, warm feeling in the congregation is illustrated by this memory, treasured by one of our narrators:

We used to have children's programs at night. Preacher Shelton was the preacher then. We were sitting over in one side, after our program was over. And Preacher Shelton got up, talking about the program, and complimented it, and said how wonderful it is to be a child. And he said what we all would have missed had we never been children. And thinking of Adam, he said, "Can any of you wonderful boys and girls tell me a man that never was a boy?" Roy held up his hand—he was my cousin—and Mr. Shelton says, "All right, Roy, you tell

*us." (He knew all of us children by name.) Roy said
(pointing to the child beside him), "Louise Mann." Oh,
that was so funny. Everybody was laughing. Preacher
Shelton said that knocked his speech out of him.*

Each child in the congregation participated in these church
programs, which provided public speaking experience for
those who took part and good entertainment for the
listeners.

The church also provided the only means most people
had for observing the world outside of their village. Every
year the church sponsored a trip to the state fair in Raleigh.
The Sunday school classes also held annual excursions;
sometimes they went by train to Hillsborough (twenty miles
away) to picnic on the mill owner's estate. These occasions
were the social highlights of many people's lives. Most of
our married narrators met their spouses in either the mill or
the church. The walk home after church was a great
attraction for the teenagers:

*We had a training union then. After that was over, we'd
meet on Sunday afternoon. We would all, just a bunch of
us, get together and go out. Maybe we'd walk down to
Chapel Hill. Or, in the summertime, we went just out in
the country. You know, just enjoying a walk. Had a good
time.*

But the narrow borders of the village, comfortable and
secure for the small child, sometimes turned into
constricting limits for a restless adolescent. The community
offered very little in the way of education and held out few
options for employment and life-style. Nearly everyone in
town worked in the mill; the exceptions—doctor, preacher,
storekeeper—were seen as models beyond most people's
reach. When we asked our narrators what they, as
children, had dreamed of being when they grew up, none
could remember having any aspirations. Did a yearning for
something beyond the daily round of ordinary life break
through at certain moments? One of our narrators
described a poignant and vivid image of her father which
seemed to embody for her this "dreaming" mood:

He'd lay his cheek over on that violin and close his eyes, you know, and play "The Devil's Dream." It seemed like he dreamed over his playing. I don't know why. He'd come in before time to have dinner—supper, we called it then, of course, still do—and he'd get his fiddle out, and he'd stand and play so dreamily.

TWENTY-SEVEN
Saturday Night at the Mall

ALMA BLOUNT

TAMMY IS SEVENTEEN
and Johnny just turned twenty. They've been married for two years and live with Johnny's parents. Johnny works a forty-hour week at American Threshold Company, where he runs cloth off a squirrel cage and cuts it with a skillsaw so that it can be made into those small rugged blue towels that car mechanics use. Tammy is a part-time lifeguard at the Little Red Play School. Gene, Johnny's cousin, is seventeen years old.

Johnny is well respected in the group of twenty or so regulars who hang out at the mall, in the back section. Several other groups from other schools or sections of town hang out in the front of the mall—and everyone there knows who Johnny and Tammy are—but Johnny has the most power and esteem.

JOHNNY: BEING FRIENDS IS
really what it's all about. We'll come up here, circle around a time or two, show the car off.

We try to keep peace. But if we get out here and anybody starts any shit, we fight, ya know. We're not afraid of nobody or nothing like that.

Sometimes people come up here and they get too drunk, and they say something about the car, like they say it won't run. And you go out and get in a drag race, and they lose. Say they get mad 'cause they lose. So instead of giving you **245**

The Mall by Day

*the money they owe you for racing if you won, they
want to fight about it. So you end up getting into a fight.*

*Or sometimes someone comes around and hollers at
her—and she's my wife—hollers hey baby you want to do
all this bunch of junk, and all like that, and I'll jump their
case for that, 'cause I don't want anybody messing
around with my wife like that.*

*I ain't in trouble with the law no more. I've been in
trouble too many times, been throwed behind bars too
many times. I've been too damn bad, been a damn mean
ass is what the hell I've been.*

TAMMY: *But he's straightened up a lot. I'm proud of him.*

JOHNNY: *I've straightened my ass up. I'm on three years'
probation. I'm trying to do what the hell's right. I've got
a damn job. I'm just around here partying normal, raising
hell. I'm trying to do what's right.*

*I've been coming up here ever since I was sixteen, ever
since I was old enough to drive. I'm twenty now. I'll
probably be coming up here till I'm too old to walk.*

*I dread to get old, man, 'cause I'm going to miss like
hell bein' up here.*

*See, when you come up here every weekend, there's
always different things you can do. But you got to be a
survivor to find it. If you don't find it, there ain't going to
be nothing to do.*

GENE: *I'VE BEEN ON MY OWN SINCE I WAS ELEVEN YEARS* old. I've carried a knife all my damn life.

I've been in trouble with my family and everything, gotten into fights with them and all this stuff, got ran out of the house. I've been raised in motorcycle gangs and all this other good stuff. And I always carry a knife and a set of brass knucks. I always have.

Well, I sold a set of brass knucks tonight. But I wish I hadn't a now. But I got the blade, and I ain't worried about it. I ain't never had to use the knife but one time, and I hope I don't never have to use it again. But the first time I ever used a knife, it was all to hell, I'll tell ya that right now.

I was in a beer joint, and this guy walked up to me, said he was going to bust my skull. And the only chance I had was to use the knife or get my head busted. Now if a guy says he's going to bust your skull and you ain't but eleven years old, you ain't got no choice.

A DRUNK WOMAN WHO LOOKED LIKE SHE WAS TWENTY-five or thirty years old was screaming and kicking at Gene

and Johnny. Finally her male companion, who also looked like he was thirty, forced her into her car and took her away.

JOHNNY: *SHE WAS MAD 'CAUSE GENE PULLED THE COIL WIRE OFF so she wouldn't go out and get herself killed in her car 'cause she was too drunk and she was mad at something. So she started pushing Gene around and drew her knife, and I said, "You're going to have to cut me before you cut anybody." And she started kicking me, and I just grabbed the knife and took it away from her.*

She said she was going to get a gun next. I said, "Well, the first person you shoot," I said, "make it me," I said, " 'cause you ain't going to shoot none of my friends."

Stuff like that happens about regular. It's something every weekend. Either it's a dude or a girl. You just got to stand your ground and hold on. If we get killed we get killed, and if we don't we don't.

TWENTY-EIGHT
Annie Milson's Adventure

DOROTHY WILLIAMS, AGE 8, 1938

CHAPTER ONE:
The Large Room

ONCE UPON A TIME, there was a little girl whose name was Annie Milson. This little girl lived in Althea, Georgia. Now, one day Annie was walking toward town, which led by the cruel people's house. A woman was leaning out of a window and, when Annie went past the window, the woman reached out and picked her (Annie, I mean, of course!) up! She took her into a large room where there was nothing in the world but some old chests and a few shelves on which were some bottles. Over to one of the chests she went and took out an old torn-up dress and put it on top of the chest. Then she took a bottle from one of the shelves and started toward Annie! Now, of course, you have decided that the woman was crazy, but she wasn't. The woman (whose name was Mrs. Higgens) said to Annie, "Come here, you brat."

Annie obeyed. She was too frightened to do otherwise. Mrs. Higgens undressed her and poured something that stung from the bottle onto her head. She then dressed her in that awful dress and led her to the door!

CHAPTER TWO

Work or Be Whipped

POOR ANNIE! SHE HAD BEEN SNATCHED INTO A STRANGE
house by a strange woman. Mrs. Higgens opened the door
and led her through it. There in the other room (which was
also very large) were many sinks, towels, and safes. On
each sink were many dishes, some soap, and a rag. Mrs.
Higgens rang a bell, and a lot of little girls (who, like Annie,
had been grabbed from the street) came running in and
looked at Annie with pitying eyes. One of the girls came
over to Annie and told her this: "Mrs. Higgens gives us a
certain length of time to wash, dry, and put away all these
dishes, and if we aren't through when she comes in, we
are whipped with that buggy whip you see over there on
the wall. Come with me." Annie felt better, for this girl was
friendly. She went with the girl (Alice by name) and soon
found herself busy washing dishes at a sink. Annie was
putting away her last dish when Mrs. Higgens appeared.
One girl was not through and began to hurry and broke
one of them. Annie pitied her. She whispered to the girl at
the next sink, "Does Mrs. Higgens run it by herself?" The
girl told her, "Yes, she runs it by herself. She wouldn't
have anybody else. The Meany."

CHAPTER THREE

Annie's Roommate

NIGHT CAME AT LAST, AND ANNIE WAS GLAD TO GO TO A
little cabin where she was to stay. There she found Alice,
who said, "I am going to be your roommate. Tonight I will
tell you some of the things we do here." Annie listened to
her tell of the many things they did in that terrible place.
After awhile they began to get sleepy and went to bed. The
next morning, they had an egg for breakfast. "You see,
Mrs. Higgens does try to keep us fit for the work by an egg
for breakfast," said Alice. Then they went out to play, for

they did not only have to work there. They played most of the morning, and about ten o'clock they washed their dishes. Nobody was slow today. This went on for two whole weeks. Then something happened. I will save it for another chapter though.

CHAPTER FOUR
Another Horrible Place

EARLY ONE MORNING, ANNIE WAS STANDING AT THE DOOR of her cabin. A big truck drove up to the front gate. Soon Mrs. Higgens came out to them and told them to get in the truck. Soon they were riding along well-known roads to the country. Finally, they came to Baileyville, and soon the man in the truck drove up a driveway and stopped. A woman came out of the house and looked at them and asked something about how much Annie and Alice would cost. She took them out and into the house. She told poor Annie and Alice that they were to be her maids. And so they were for a month. Always doing hard work and meekly obeying her orders, poor souls.

CHAPTER FIVE
A Blessed Man

ONE AFTERNOON ANNIE WAS IN THE KITCHEN MAKING some delicious sandwiches when suddenly Alice exclaimed, "Annie, here he comes." For the mistress of the house was to have company that afternoon, and he was now riding up. Their mistress ran to meet him, and they came back to the house. As soon as the young gentleman saw them, he exclaimed, "Why, Mary," and began muttering something about she shouldn't have white little girls for maids and that he was going to do something about it. He asked, "Who are you little girls and where did you come from?" "I am Annie Milson and this is my friend Alice Palmer, and we come from Althea,'' said Annie in an excited tone of voice before Alice had time to say a word.

CHAPTER SIX

Home Again

THE GOOD MAN ASKED THEM MANY QUESTIONS. HE GAVE them good clothes and each a horse to go home on. They gave him many thanks and started on their way. Soon they

arrived home, and Annie with a thankful heart ran straight into her mother's arms for the first time since that awful day when she was going to town. Mrs. Milson planned a big dinner for the celebration of her daughter's return. They would have many friends and relatives to their dinner and in the afternoon would do and play many things. Roast apples, nuts, and marshmallows and pop popcorn. Ask riddles and play cards. Finally, the day came. Annie was up at an early hour. Their many guests arrived. In the afternoon, when the guests were leaving, they carried Annie and Alice in turn up on their shoulders and threw flowers at them and shouted, "Three cheers for two

Sunday School Graduation at the First Baptist Church, East Texas

adventurous girls!'' And that night Annie said to her mother, ''I shall never go past that house anymore, and if I do, I will walk on the other side of the street.'' And with that she fell asleep.

THE END

TWENTY-NINE

The First Day: Little Rock, 1957

ELIZABETH ECKFORD, WITH DAISY BATES

ON MAY 17, 1954, THE United States Supreme Court ruled in the case of Brown v. Board of Education *that the concept of "separate but equal" facilities—long used to justify segregated public school systems in the nation, particularly in the South—was unconstitutional. Across the South, school systems immediately began to react to the ruling. A few complied readily with the new law of the land; some issued vehement statements of defiance; others simply dragged out the process of desegregation as long as they could without openly thwarting the court's ruling.*

The response of the school administrators in Little Rock, Arkansas, was typical of the middle-of-the-road, foot-dragging reaction. The Little Rock school board decided to begin desegregation at the high school level, and they planned to introduce a hand-picked group of nine black students into previously all-white Central High School, in the fall of 1957.

The situation in Little Rock was deceptively promising. In a school board election in 1956, Little Rock voters had voiced their apparent support of the gradual desegregation plan by defeating two rabidly segregationist candidates in favor of two moderates. In the governor's race, the fiery racist Jim Johnson had failed in his challenge to the incumbent— supposedly moderate Orval Faubus.

257

The first day of the 1957–58 school term was scheduled for September 3, the day after Labor Day. In a surprise move late on Labor Day afternoon, Governor Faubus called out the Arkansas National Guard to prevent the nine black students from entering Central High the next day. The school board then requested that "no Negro students attempt to enter Central or any other white high school until this dilemma is legally resolved." None did. On Tuesday, the federal district court ruled that the desegregation plan be carried out as usual.

On Wednesday, September 4, the nine black teenagers attempted for the first time to enter Central High, which was now surrounded by National Guard troops and an angry segregationist mob. Eight of the black students were accompanied by the city police and a group of concerned adults. But fifteen-year-old Elizabeth Eckford had somehow not been notified of the group's plans, and approached the school alone. Her encounter with the hostile crowd and the National Guard blazed across the wire services that evening, focusing the world's attention on Little Rock.

THAT NIGHT I WAS SO EXCITED I COULDN'T SLEEP. THE NEXT morning I was about the first one up. While I was pressing my black-and-white dress—I had made it to wear on the first day of school—my little brother turned on the TV set. They started telling about a large crowd gathered at the school. The man on TV said he wondered if we were going to show up that morning. Mother called from the kitchen, where she was fixing breakfast, "Turn that TV off!" She was so upset and worried. I wanted to comfort her, so I said, "Mother, don't worry."

Dad was walking back and forth, from room to room, with a sad expression. He was chewing on his pipe and he had a cigar in his hand, but he didn't light either one. It would have been funny, only he was so nervous.

Before I left home Mother called us into the living room. She said we should have a word of prayer. Then I caught the bus and got off a block from the school. I saw a large crowd of people standing across the street from the soldiers guarding Central. As I walked on, the crowd suddenly got very quiet. Superintendent Blossom had told us to enter by the front door. I looked at all the people and thought, "Maybe I will be safer if I walk down the block to the front entrance behind the guards."

At the corner I tried to pass through the long line of guards around the school so as to enter the grounds behind them. One of the guards pointed across the street. So I pointed in the same direction and asked whether he meant for me to cross the street and walk down. He nodded "yes." So, I walked across the street conscious of the crowd that stood there, but they moved away from me.

For a moment all I could hear was the shuffling of their feet. Then someone shouted, "Here she comes, get ready!" I moved away from the crowd on the sidewalk and into the street. If the mob came at me I could then cross back over so the guards could protect me.

The crowd moved in closer and then began to follow me, calling me names. I still wasn't afraid. Just a little bit nervous. Then my knees started to shake all of a sudden

and I wondered whether I could make it to the center entrance a block away. It was the longest block I ever walked in my whole life.

Even so, I still wasn't too scared because all the time I kept thinking that the guards would protect me.

When I got in front of the school, I went up to a guard again. But this time he just looked straight ahead and didn't move to let me pass him. I didn't know what to do. Then I looked and saw that the path leading to the front entrance was a little further ahead. So I walked until I was right in front of the path to the front door.

I stood looking at the school—it looked so big! Just then the guards let some white students through.

The crowd was quiet. I guess they were waiting to see what was going to happen. When I was able to steady my knees, I walked up to the guard who had let the white students in. He too didn't move. When I tried to squeeze past him, he raised his bayonet and then the other guards moved in and they raised their bayonets.

They glared at me with a mean look and I was very frightened and didn't know what to do. I turned around and the crowd came toward me.

They moved closer and closer. Somebody started yelling, "Lynch her! Lynch her!"

I tried to see a friendly face somewhere in the mob— someone who maybe would help. I looked into the face of an old woman and it seemed a kind face, but when I looked at her again, she spat on me.

They came closer, shouting, "No nigger bitch is going to get in our school. Get out of here!"

I turned back to the guards but their faces told me I wouldn't get any help from them. Then I looked down the block and saw a bench at the bus stop. I thought, "If I can only get there I will be safe." I don't know why the bench seemed a safe place to me, but I started walking toward it. I tried to close my mind to what they were shouting, and kept saying to myself, "If I can only make it to the bench I will be safe."

When I finally got there, I don't think I could have gone another step. I sat down and the mob crowded up and began shouting all over again. Someone hollered, "Drag her over to this tree! Let's take care of that nigger." Just then a white man sat down beside me, put his arm around me and patted my shoulder. He raised my chin and said, "Don't let them see you cry."

THE TEXT HERE IS
*adapted from a preliminary
report profiling Southern
children, prepared by the
Southern Growth Policies
Board's Task Force on the
Status of Children in the
South. The report is available
to interested citizens and
groups in two forms, both
entitled "Raising a New
Generation in the South": (1) a
twenty-page booklet prepared
by Paula Breen and Margaret
Scarborough, and (2) a
twenty-minute slide show with
140 slides and printed
narration, prepared by Gary
Richman of Richman
Communications. The text
here was adapted by Alden
Clark. For copies of either
resource, contact Paula Breen.*

APPENDIX
Childhood in Numbers

SOUTHERN CHILDREN LIVE
in a unique environment, with
special advantages and
disadvantages rooted in the
culture and economy of the
region.* The statistics presented
here, compiled by the Southern
Growth Policies Board Task
Force on the Status of Children
in the South, provide vital

*The "South" in this report
encompasses fourteen states:
Alabama, Arkansas, Florida,
Georgia, Kentucky, Louisiana,
Mississippi, North Carolina,
Oklahoma, South Carolina,
Tennessee, Texas, Virginia and
West Virginia. When the term
"Census South" is used, it
refers to these fourteen states,
plus Maryland, Delaware and
the District of Columbia.

263

in the South, provide vital information about the nature of the world inhabited by children in today's South, and especially the extra handicaps faced by Southern poor children.

TO BEGIN WITH, THE SOUTH'S POPULATION IS YOUNGER than that of the nation as a whole. With 19.4 million children, the South has a larger portion of its population— 31 percent—under age eighteen than any other region in the country. Similarly, 7.6 percent of the South's population is under five years of age, compared to 6.8 percent in the non-South. Future projections indicate that growth in the South will continue to make us even younger compared to the rest of the nation. The South's birth rate, although declining, is still higher than the rate in other regions. The South is also growing through the migration of new Southerners, who tend to be young adults with growing families. From 1970 to 1978, migration alone accounted for increases in the school-age population in almost every Southern state, ranging from 1.4 percent in Alabama to 17 percent in Florida.

THE NEWEST SOUTHERN ARRIVAL, THE INFANT, IS BORN with a poorer chance of surviving his or her first year of life than other children in the U.S. While rates of infant death have decreased significantly nationwide and in the South, the gap between the South and the rest of the nation has not appreciably narrowed. In 1975 the number of deaths in the first year of life was 17.8 per thousand live births in the South, 15.3 in the non-South. The figure for non-whites is even more striking: 27.9 per thousand in the South, compared to 21.7 in other regions. Risk factors associated with infant mortality such as low birth weight and teenage pregnancy occur more frequently in the South. And although modern medical technology has increased the survival rate of very tiny infants, these babies, and those born to teenage mothers, remain at high risk for lifelong handicapping conditions. In fact, estimates of the handicapped population indicate that the South has a slightly higher percentage of handicapped children. Underlying all the factors of infant mortality, especially the dramatically worse statistics for non-white children, is the grim reality of poverty.

A CHILD IN THE SOUTH IS FAR MORE LIKELY TO GROW up in poverty than is a child in another region. The South is home to 30 percent of the nation's children, but 40 percent of the country's poor children and 45 percent of desperately poor children (family earnings below 75 percent of poverty level) live here.

The first five years of life are extremely important in human development, and the effects of poverty are most devastating then. Lack of adequate nutrition, health care, and other basic needs during these years may lead to physical and/or psychological problems which persist later in life, causing many children to follow in the poverty cycle of their parents. The number and proportion of children in poor families has declined since 1969, but the rate of poverty for pre-school children remains unchanged. Almost one million Southern children under five years old live in families classified as poor.

One of the accompaniments of poverty is poor housing, and the numbers show that the houses in which Southern children grow up are more likely to be of inferior quality. Plumbing facilities (a measure often used to indicate substandard housing) were lacking in 13 percent of "white dwelling units" and 32.1 percent of "black dwelling units" in the Census South in 1970, compared to 3.2 percent of white units and 4.8 percent of black units in the rest of the country.

ALTHOUGH THERE IS A GREATER CONCENTRATION OF children growing up in poverty in the South, Southern children receive less financial assistance from available public resources, such as Aid to Families with Dependent Children (AFDC) and Medicaid. For example, in 1975 less than 2 million of the South's 4 million poor children received AFDC cash benefits while nationally 8 million children were enrolled in the program compared with a total of 10 million poor children. Because AFDC has complex eligibility rules which vary from state to state, these figures do not represent a precisely comparable participation rate for the program. But they do show that, statistically, a poor child in the South is less likely to receive income assistance than a poor child in the rest of the country. Moreover, because AFDC benefit levels established by states in the South are lower (an average of $64 per month for a Southern child in 1979 compared to $142 for a child in the non-South), the maximum AFDC and Food Stamp benefit package is correspondingly lower than the U.S. median. Ironically, the federal share of that combined benefit package ranges from 70 to 96 percent in the South.

Analysis of Medicaid benefits for children shows similar trends. Forty percent of the nation's poor children live in the South, but only 22 percent of the child Medicaid recipients are Southern. And in most Southern states the average Medicaid expenditure for each child in 1976 was significantly lower than the $240 per year national average, even though 67 percent of the South's Medicaid bill is paid by Washington as opposed to 49 percent for the rest of the nation.

THE CYCLE OF POVERTY IS IN PART PERPETUATED AND IN part reflected by deficiencies in education. The school dropout rate in the South is 50 percent higher than elsewhere; out of 880,000 American dropouts examined in one study in 1975–76, 300,000 had been enrolled in Southern schools. Moreover, 42 percent of the nation's children enrolled in grades behind their age-group live in the South. Throughout the 1970s, Southern students improved their scores on standardized achievement tests, especially in the area of reading, but test scores of children in the South remain below the national average.

The causes of these statistics, like those for infant mortality rates, are varied. One factor in the educational lag of Southern children is that their parents tend to have less formal education. Forty-two percent of parents in the Census South did not finish high school, compared to 34 percent in the U.S. More importantly, total per pupil expenditures for Southern students are significantly less than in the rest of the nation: $1,468 versus $2,010. As in the case of AFDC benefits, the South gets more per student from the federal government but invests less state and local tax money. Local contribution to education is $527 per pupil compared to over $1,000 in the U.S. as a whole.

THE NUMBERS DESCRIBING THE SOUTHERN CHILDHOOD are not all negative. One advantage Southern children enjoy is closer family ties. More Southern children live within walking distance to other relatives than children in any other region of the country, and fewer Southern children live in single-parent homes than do children in the non-South: in 1975, 83.7 percent lived in homes with both their mother and father.

Close proximity to extended families can provide women with a network of support in sharing child-raising responsibilities, a network that can be more positive and inexpensive than the custodial care provided in some day-care centers. The need for day care is also greater in the region since more mothers are in the workforce than elsewhere. They work whether they are single parents or whether they live with their husbands. They are entering the job market in increasing numbers, with the greatest increases among mothers of children under age three. The latest figures show that nearly half—48.5 percent—of all Southern mothers with pre-school children work outside the home. This includes about 45 percent of women who live with their husbands and two-thirds of the women who head single-parent families—a higher percentage in each case than for women living in other regions of the country.

FEW WOULD DENY THAT THE FUTURE OF THE SOUTH IS inevitably tied to the care and welfare of our young, but who will take responsibility? And what measures will be taken? Can the South's disproportionate burden of poverty be alleviated without sacrificing the unique cultural vision, without relinquishing deep-rooted Southern values such as the importance of kinship and place? The preceding statistical profile points out other issues policy makers and Southern citizens must address in facing the challenge of a new generation. Other concerns for which comparable regional data is lacking, but which also require attention, include the special needs of handicapped children; migrant and immigrant children; abused children; delinquent children; children living out of their homes, especially those lost in foster care; children with alcohol and drug problems; bilingual children as well as gifted and talented children.

For more information about the work of the Task Force on the Status of Children in the South, contact Paula Breen, Southern Growth Policies Board, P.O. Box 12293, Research Triangle Park, North Carolina 27709.

Photography Credits

Grateful acknowledgment is made to the following for supplying or allowing the use of photographs:

Nathalie Andrews: p. 217, p. 219, pp. 220–21
Alma Blount: pp. 246–49
Robert Cooper: pp. 45–50
Tom Davenport: p. 34
Belton Gray: p. 182
Alferdteen Harrison: pp. 70–71
Bernard Herrman: p. 162, p. 167
Lerner Family: p. 79
Library of Congress: p. 4, p. 38, p. 214
Leslie Lilly: p. 106, p. 118, p. 139
Stephen March: p. ii
North Carolina State Archives: p. 230, p. 239
Melva Okun: p. 146
Nathan Pierson: p. 259
Portland Museum, Portland, Kentucky: pp. 217–18
Thordis Simonsen: pp. 10–11, pp. 13–14, p. 16, p. 19, p. 21, p. 26, p. 74, p. 191 (© 1980 Thordis Simonsen)
Slone Family: p. 28
Allan Troxler: p. 155, p. 157
Wendy Watriss, Fred Baldwin: p. 41, p. 54, p. 78, p. 88, p. 172–73, p. 254–55 (© 1980 Wendy Watriss/Fred Baldwin)
Marie Wood: p. 64, p. 89

About the Contributors

Nathalie Andrews is interim director of the Portland Museum at the Roosevelt Community School in Louisville, Kentucky.

Alma Blount works as a freelance photographer in North Carolina.

Will D. Campbell, known to his friends as "Preacher Will," lives on a farm outside Mt. Juliet, Tennessee.

Robert Cooper is currently an M.F.A. student at Rochester Institute of Technology. His personal photography has been published in *Appalachia: A Self-Portrait*, by Appalshop, Inc., Whitesburg, Ky., 1979.

Dwight Childers is a North Carolina poet.

Karen Fields is Mamie Garvin Fields's granddaughter and her editor. The two are preparing a book, *Lemon Swap and Other Places: A Black Woman Remembers*.

Danny Gafford is now twenty-four years old. He has been imprisoned on Florida's death row for the past five years.

Larry Goodwyn teaches history at Duke University.

Ann Green is a former student in Sea Chest, a project of the Cape Hatteras School in Buxton, N.C., on Carolina's Outer Banks. The Project publishes *Sea Chest*, a biannual magazine.

Joyce Green lives in Bartow, Georgia.

Shelia Gunder lives in Louisville, Georgia.

Alferdteen Harrison, a Mississippian who attented Piney Woods School, is director of the Institute for the Study of the History, Life and Culture of Black People at Jackson State University in Jackson, Mississippi.

Lanier Rand Holt has worked for the past three years on the staff of Duke University's Center for the Study of the Family and the State in Durham, North Carolina.

Robert Houston has worked as a steelworker, librarian, actor, junior executive and sandwich truck-driver. He now teaches writing at the University of Arizona.

Honoree F. Jeffers lives in Durham, North Carolina.

Ruby Lerner is now the director of Alternate ROOTS, a coalition of community-based theater and dance companies and individual artists across the South.

John Lewis was chairman of SNCC for several years and then director of the Voter Registration Project. He now works for the National Consumer Cooperative Bank.

Wekesa Madzimoyo is a former staff member of the Institute for Southern Studies. Currently he works as a community organizer and trainer for FOCAL (Federation of Child Care Centers of Alabama).

Chris Mayfield edited this book and is a staff member of the Institute for Southern Studies, which publishes *Southern Exposure.*

Ricky McArthur lives in Beaufort County, South Carolina.

Michael Bert McCarthy, who calls himself a "subversive ex-convict," was an original writer on the Emmy-award-winning *Jericho Mile*, and is currently at work on a television movie and novel on prison themes. He lives in Los Angeles.

Amelia Midgett is a former student in the *Sea Chest* project.

Jennifer Miller is an editor and writer, and has worked with the Institute for Southern Studies for the past five years.

Margie O'Brien lives in Beaufort County, South Carolina.

Angie Perry lives in Durham, North Carolina.

Valerie Quinney teaches history at the at the University of Rhode Island.

Steve Roberts was born on Portsmouth Island on North Carolina's Outer Banks in 1901, and lived there until his family moved to the mainland when he was eleven years old.

Thomasine Roper lives in Durham, North Carolina.

Rick Scarborough is a former student in the *Sea Chest* project.

Mab Segrest is a lesbian-feminist poet and a critic. She grew up in Alabama in the 1950s and currently works on *Feminary: A Feminist Journal for the South.*

Jim Sessions is executive director of Southerners for Economic Justice.

Thordis Simonsen teaches courses in biology and cultural change at the Kent Denver School in Denver, Colorado.

Verna Mae Slone lives in Pippa Passes, Kentucky.

Caroline Smith is a former student in the *Sea Chest* project.

Sue Thrasher is a former staff member of *Southern Exposure*. She is currently on the staff of the Highlander Research and Education Center.

Allan Troxler, who grew up in Greensboro, North Carolina, is co-director of the Institute of Southern Studies' *Our South* project. He aims to do a book for children one of these days.

Allen Tullos is a graduate student in the folklore department at the University of North Carolina at Chapel Hill.

Antonio Walker lives in Durham, North Carolina.

Dorothy Williams teaches second grade in Macom, Georgia.

7-1-81
2